Colyto

The story of wartime in the country
told from the memories of East Devon
men and women

By Geoff Elliott

Published by the
Colyton Parish History Society

For Lyn, who ensured deadlines would be met

Published 2007 by the Colyton Parish History Society

Copyright © Geoff Elliott 2007

ISBN 978-0-9556743-0-3

Printed and bound by Creeds the Printers, of Broadoak, Bridport, Dorset

Illustrations by Andrea Martin

About the Colyton Parish History Society

Colyton Parish History Society was founded in 1986 and now has 130 members. A series of winter talks are held, often illustrated, and in the summer visits to places of historical interest are arranged. Escorted tours of the town and St Andrew's Church are available for groups on request.

The society has premises in Colyton car park, half being occupied by the Service Point, administered by the society on behalf of the Devon Record Office, where members of the public can research their family or property history and where there is access to census records and trade directories etc. This facility is open Thursday afternoons from 2 to 5pm. The other half houses a collection of deeds, documents, books, photographs and maps. This is open every weekday from 2 to 4.30pm, Easter to October.

If you can add to this archive about Colyton at War, or have any other interest in contacting us, please do so through our website, www.colytonhistory.co.uk

Shirley Campbell Brown, chairman

About the author

 Geoff Elliott was the editor of three newspapers, including the Coventry Evening Telegraph and the Portsmouth Evening News. Later, he became head of the Department of Journalism at the University of Central Lancashire. In turn, he was a member of the Press Complaints Commission and the Broadcasting Standards Commission. He was the founding president of the Society of Editors in 1999 and is now a fellow. In 2004, he was appointed CBE for services to journalism. He lives at Umborne, near Colyton.

Contents

Contents continued

Contents continued

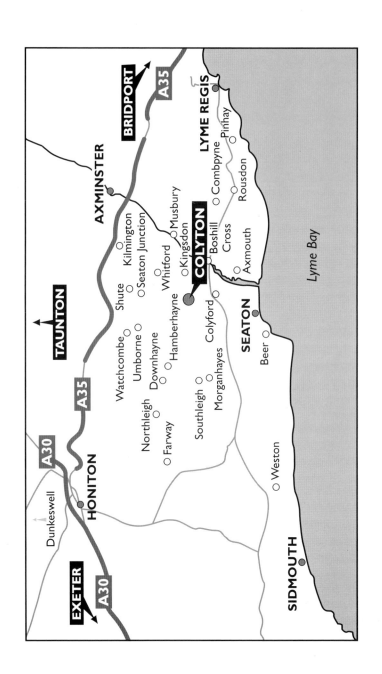

Introduction

A single bomb fell on Colyton during the Second World War. It was an incendiary and it came through the roof of the railway station. It caused a small hole and no more.

Seaton was less fortunate. Nine of its people and two evacuees, escaping supposedly more dangerous areas, died in hit-and-run bombing raids.

Yet the price of war for the two communities, and the towns and villages around them in East Devon, was tiny compared with the misery and devastation heaped on the inhabitants of some of Britain's cities.

In many ways, life went on much as before. Colyton was a rural idyll, a self-sufficient little town in the middle of generous countryside. It was a land of plenty, not only for the locals but for the many others who became its guests.

For there were also evacuees to feed. There were billeted soldiers, first British troops retreating from Dunkirk, then later others preparing in camps for the D-Day invasion. There were Czechs and Poles and finally Americans. There were Land Army girls, and even prisoners-of-war.

Here are the stories of some of Colyton's people, young then in wartime, told in words they might have used themselves.

They cover the dramatic events and the mundane, collectively creating a vivid picture, not only of Colyton at war but also of other parts of East Devon.

So turn back the clock to years slipping beyond our memories, to a war that for most in this happy place was also a happy time, hosts and visitors seeing the very best in one another.

Evacuees marching with garden forks to Dig for Victory

Country Lives at War

Barbara Land

He looked in our hair, and poked and prodded us. We were really quite indignant about it all. We felt like commodities being tested to see if we were still fresh and wholesome

Mothers were barred from the station platform unless they were travelling with their children. They had to shed their tears behind the railings as their children skipped excitedly to the trains.

My own mother was one of them. In the middle of a chaotic crowd of women grieving already for children they were losing to the countryside, she hugged me and kissed me goodbye. Then, red-eyed, she waved desperately as I passed through the gates.

I was with my aunt because our local council had decided to permit mothers evacuating the capital with a child under three years of age to take three other children with them. So my school had left London without me, bound for Norfolk.

We all had to meet at another school in Walworth, from where we were taken by coach with our bundles and bags to Waterloo Station for our journey to a safer place.

Having been labelled to say who we were and where we had come from, we got on our train. At the age of eight, it was the most thrilling day of my young life. Perched on my seat in the carriage, I hadn't the inkling of an idea where I was going.

Somewhere among my luggage would have been my gas mask, a fearful addition to my belongings, because we had been instructed to take it everywhere we went. Some people had them in fancy bags or little cases to disguise their unpleasantness.

Even as we chugged out of London and down the track towards our destination, we had no idea where we were. All the signs bearing the names of the places in which we stopped had been taken down so any invaders wouldn't know where they were – or at least that was the idea.

At Salisbury people gave us tea and snacks through the windows because we had nothing with us.

Eventually, they told us we had reached Seaton Junction where we were to get off the train, and it was here that we were sorted into groups for onward journeys to particular villages and towns. This sorting process took place in the Express Dairies depot. There, we were given milk and biscuits, not the lemonade children might have expected, and a brown carrier bag containing a tin of corned beef, a tin of condensed milk and some chocolate. Everyone had these bags, children and adults alike. It was as if these were to be our rations for the whole of our stay in the countryside.

We moved along as we were told, and now on to our coach that was to take my aunt, my cousin, Kitty, and my friends, Helen and Rita, to Colyton. Our sanctuary in the countryside.

Here we were to spend much of the war very happily, even if our first taste of country ways was not very appetising. For, on the stage at the far end of the town hall stood the doctor, and in front of him, local dignitaries including Mrs Tyson, the billeting officer.

First, we had to report to the doctor. Our names were called out and we had to go up the steps for an examination. He looked in our hair and listened to our chests, and poked and prodded us. We were really quite indignant about it all. I suppose we felt like commodities being tested to see if we were still fresh and wholesome. After the doctor had finished with us, we were sent back to our seats to wait. When the call came it was for the 'lady with four children'. That was us. We were told we were going to stay on a farm called Hamberhayne and that the farmers were Ida and Edward Summers, who had no children.

The farm was about three miles away, and, like the others, we were taken to our new homes by car. Scouts were on hand to help us with our luggage, as nervously we boarded the car that had been pointed out to us. At Hamberhayne, we clambered out again and were led into a large house, part of which had been set aside for us. The first shock was to find there was neither electricity nor gas. We had been used to both in London, but now we were to have oil lamps for light and an oil stove, more like a Primus stove, for cooking. And water came from a pump across the yard. My aunt hardly knew whether she was coming or going, and for a time we got used to cold beans and potatoes. But we had nice bedrooms, and the stove was set in a little kitchen just for us.

One day Ida cooked us rabbit stew. Everyone around here seemed to eat a lot of that. I guess there were so many rabbits for the taking. But I'd never eaten it before, and I was a bit apprehensive of doing so now. The only rabbits I had ever known were pretty, furry, little things you kept as pets.

It wasn't long before we wanted to go to town, but it was such a long way. We weren't used to walking distances like that. We borrowed a pushchair from the next farm and set off. Kitty started in the pushchair, but it wasn't long before we were taking it in turns. We found it absolutely exhausting. But the reward came in the sweets my aunt bought for us from a little shop.

For now, there was no question of our going to school. Then St Jude's, the school also evacuated from London, had use of the school buildings in the morning, and the local council school had them in the afternoon. They swapped over every week. Before attending school, first Kitty and then Helen had scarlet fever. They had caught it, apparently, drinking out of the same cups as other people on the train from London. They were both isolated in hospital at Exeter. One day, we went to see them. Nobody travelled very much in those days, and though we had come much farther from London it was still quite a trek. We had to catch the little train to Seaton Junction and then the mainline train to Exeter.

However, when Kitty and Helen were discharged, the rest of us were not allowed to be in the same house, so Rita and I had to move out. We were taken to Colyton and lived with a Miss Turl and her father. That's when we started to go to school with the local children, mornings one week, afternoons the next. The school consisted of two big classrooms, each having a curtain that could be pulled across to divide the room. When that was done, we might not have been able to see the other teacher and the children, but we could certainly hear what was going on, though we tried to take no notice of it. In the winter, two big stoves kept us warm.

Out in the playground in the mornings, a whistle would call us to attention. We formed up in line and marched in to music, with the headmaster, Mr Jenkins, standing at the door, beating time. There was such a rhythmic clatter as the boys, in their big farm boots, thudded out time to Mr Jenkins's direction as they entered school.

We weren't there long because all was quiet back in London. It was the phoney war, the time when war didn't seem so bad after all. There didn't seem much point in our being away, so we went home.

When the blitz started, however, Auntie Ida, as she became known to us, invited us back to Devon. This time, my friends went to Wales with their family, but my aunt, my cousin and I returned to Hamberhayne Farm, where we stayed for three years.

There, later, we were joined by my mother and my new sister Sue, then two weeks old. It was the start of a long and happy association with Auntie Ida, one that for a while saw four generations of my family staying at the farm.

Our friendship never waned.

Barbara Land went back to the London after leaving school at the end of the war. She trained as a clerk at the Woolwich dockyard, married, had two children of her own and later worked as a bank clerk. She now lives in retirement at Gillingham in Kent.

Boys from London preparing a field in Colyton for sowing

 **Denis Swann**

He saw the cockerel glowing eerily golden in the moonlight over St Andrew's Church and a German plane flying low over the town. He was on the next train out.

We had never seen cows, nor even a green hill. We had come from Southwark, in London, where all was buildings and pavements and street noise. We had never been anywhere else. Now there were fields all around us and as many cows as you would ever want to see.

There were 100 of us, all from St Jude's Church of England School opposite the Imperial War Museum, at the start of . . . well, we didn't know what.

We had been wrenched from our homes near the Elephant and Castle on Friday, 1 September, two days before Mr Chamberlain declared war, having received no response to the British ultimatum over Poland. We had been parted from our parents and marched like an army platoon to Waterloo Station with our gas masks, our little cases, our sandwiches and the labels tied to us.

Now, here we were walking up the steps of the town hall in Colyton, as if in a dream.

Ernie Bassett and I left with a lady from Three Sycamores, a junction in the lanes towards Umborne. Outside she had a little sit-up-and-beg Ford into which we piled with our few belongings. And off we went to a life we could never have imagined on Harold and Amy Pearcy's farm at Higher Watchcombe.

I was 11 and a long way from home.

For the first month of our new lives we were let off school – I suppose to allow us to find our bearings. I remember being very inquisitive about all that was happening on the farm. To see a cow being milked was astonishingly exciting. I had never considered where milk came from. There it always was, in bottles, on the doorstep. To discover that it had actually been drawn from an animal on a faraway farm was almost beyond belief.

Going back to school came quickly enough. The trouble was we didn't know where to go. School was to be in Colyton, but where was that? Follow the telegraph poles, we were told, and off we set. It turned out to be three and a half miles there and three and a half miles back, not at all what we had been used to. After a while, my parents sent me my roller-skates. None of the locals had ever seen roller-skates before so they were quite a curiosity. Now the journey downhill to school was easy, but it was still a trudge back to the farm again. And of course once the wheels had worn out, that was that. There was no replacing them.

School was in the town hall, where my first acquaintance with Colyton had been made. We were still St Jude's, with the same teachers, and with the same headmaster, Mr George Lancaster, but in a very different place. Classes for the older children were in each corner of the hall, with infants on the stage. In the circumstances, we had to keep quiet and we did. One look from a teacher was all that it took to keep discipline. Two afternoons a week we walked up to the school allotment at the top of Sidmouth Road for our contribution to the Dig for Victory effort. Everyone enjoyed that. At the bottom of the hill was a little sweet shop where sometimes I would buy a few sweets with money from a postal order sent by mum. Another day the boys went for woodwork lessons in a yard opposite the Soanes garage.

We got on well with the local boys, who went to the council school. There was never any trouble, though we did try hard to beat them at football and cricket.

Out of school there was so much to get used to. The changing seasons, with all the jobs on a farm that follow them, matter so much more in the country. Ploughing, of course, was done by horses; there were no tractors. Haymaking was a special time of the year; cream teas would be brought to those at work in the fields. Later in the summer I would have to keep the heifers away from the apples in the orchard.

Ernie Bassett stayed at Higher Watchcombe for only six months. I was there for two or three years until my mother came with my sister to live in Colyton. They had an upstairs room in a little cottage opposite the Gerrard Arms. In the yard, I remember, there was a toilet for the whole row of cottages. There wasn't room for me with my mother but I was moved nearby to Mrs Carnell's in Hillhead.

My father stayed in London but he came for holidays. On one visit he was apparently more scared than he had ever been in London. In his night-shirt, standing at the window, my father saw the weather-vane cockerel glowing golden in the moonlight over St Andrew's Church and then a German plane flying low over the town. It must have been an eerie sight. The following day he packed and was on the next train out. He said he felt safer in his underground shelter back home.

Even for him there were compensations from life in the country. There were eggs for a start. People could not get them in London. Whenever he and other visitors came to Colyton they would take back a dozen as well as other fresh food. There never seemed to be a shortage of anything.

Evacuees at a picnic in Colyton. St Jude's headmaster George Lancaster stands centre left and billeting officer Mrs Tyson wears a hat in the background

We were happy so far from the terrible things that were happening in many of the cities. People carried on as they had always done. News of distant events reached Colyton by wireless; one of my jobs was to keep it flowing by taking the accumulator for recharging at a garage where the car park is now and collecting it again later. The war came closer when Exeter was bombed so badly and when people's sons and daughters came home on leave with awful tales to tell.

Then Colyton swelled again. In addition to evacuees there were now Americans arriving in readiness for D-Day. They camped in a field near the grammar school and some were billeted in local houses. They drank the pubs dry, all six of them. At the Bear on Chantry Bridge, where I would play darts after I had left school, the landlord would allow customers to drink only two pints of cider. It was a killer and the Americans weren't used to it. The military police would arrive and throw the drunken soldiers into the back of a wagon.

Like us, the Americans were tolerated well. They brought a different kind of life to the town. Most people had horse-drawn buggies, but the soldiers had jeeps in which they would take the local girls to dances in the town hall and in Axminster. The girls loved it. But there wasn't much for the soldiers to do. To pass the time, some of them would pull on their baseball gloves and throw balls to one another in the street beside the Colcombe Castle.

My first job was on Mr Pady's farm. In the mornings I would deliver milk on a bicycle. It seems extraordinary now but I would carry two crates on the carrier and never spill a drop. Then I went to work at the tannery stripping hair from the skins and drying the sheep's wool. It was dirty work and I grew to dislike it.

Towards the end of the war I felt homesick and went home to London . . . and to the rockets now falling on the capital. The first

I saw landed at Waterloo as I arrived.

Colyton and the countryside had been a lovely place to be. I had nothing but happy memories and still don't.

Denis Swann remained in London throughout his working life, 30 years of it as a bank messenger. He frequently came back to East Devon for holidays and retired 20 years ago to Sidford, where he still lives.

Sean Day-Lewis

We went on picking apples in the sunshine. But by bedtime the fear had returned. As my mother tucked me up, I asked if she thought we would live till morning

It was already a lovely late summer's day. The sun was shining warmly, and all was peaceful in the countryside. We had been picking apples and were looking forward to a promised picnic in the garden. But, even at the age of eight, I could sense the irony of that Sunday morning in September. For a dreadful foreboding hung in the air.

We all knew what was going to happen, Pa on his favourite bench outside the window and my brother and I, cross-legged on the floor, clinging close to our mother inside the door.

The wireless, and Neville Chamberlain's fateful words at 11am, had our rapt attention. The prime minister was telling us that a state of war existed between us and Germany.

There had been no doubting what we were to hear. Cigarette cards had been putting the fear of God into me with their pictures of planes and bombs. On a trip to London during the summer I had seen barrage balloons already hoisted high and air raid shelters assembled in people's gardens. Pa had been so sure for so long about the approach of war, and it had worried me.

Three days before the broadcast our gas masks had been delivered to our cottage above Musbury. The first of the evacuees had arrived down the hill in the village. It had already begun to seem very real, and now fear gripped me. I remember thinking the Germans would know where we all were and would come to kill us.

All the same, an uneasy peace returned to our little corner of England that day. We went on picking apples and enjoyed our family picnic in the sunshine. But by bedtime, the fear had returned. As my mother tucked me up, I asked if she thought we would live till morning. Her reassurance calmed me.

We had been in Musbury for less than two years. Pa couldn't make a living from his poetry, so he was turning his hand to detective stories. His first book here under the nom-de-plume Nicholas Blake was set in and around Musbury, including Folyton, really Colyton of course.

He wasn't the sort of man to rush into the army. I think he saw himself as a coward. He thought it best to stay and fight the war with his family. That meant joining the Home Guard.

Having been with the Officer Training Corps at school and being accomplished at shooting and marching around and looking the part, he naturally thought he would take command of the men who were too old and too young for the forces and of the farmers who had to stay on the land to keep us fed. He wanted to be the figure we now know as Captain Mainwaring. Instead leadership fell to an old buffer who had been knighted in the colonial service. Being unable to march his men to the top of the hill and back again without doing himself a mischief had apparently been no disqualification, so my father set about removing him, which he did by taking an Irish whiskey with the local commander and sneaking on the old fellow's inadequacies.

Now in charge of the platoon, Pa set about recruiting his

Cecil Day-Lewis with wife Mary

comrades. In Musbury there were two pubs. One was the New Inn, now called the Golden Hind, where the gentry drank, and the other was the Red Lion, where my father as a communist was happier playing dominoes with the working men of the village. They did their best preparing for the enemy with one rifle between them until Pa had the bright idea of enrolling the local poachers with their own guns.

But they were a funny lot, just as the TV series portrayed them. People lived in their own parishes and rarely strayed outside. There would probably have been people in Musbury who had never been as far as Colyton. One chap Pa tried to recruit said: 'We don't want to fight for they buggers at Axmouth, do us?'

They didn't like getting their feet wet either. Gun emplacements were built in a defensive line from north Devon to south. Whether they were meant to keep Germans out of Devon and Cornwall or to keep them there, I don't know. But in the Axe Valley, where of course it can get very wet in winter, the emplacements were often submerged. The chaps resolutely refused to go and stand in the water up to their ankles and so they were marched off to higher ground where they would stay dry.

People believed that the Germans would invade through Seaton. Had they done so, the men, whatever they lacked in skills or weapons, would have confronted the enemy, for they would have been fighting for their own place. Yet they would assuredly have been brushed aside.

In his autobiography, *The Buried Day* (Chatto and Windus, 1960), my father wrote fondly about them. He had brought his family to the Axe Valley and he remembers his feelings and his insecurity as his Home Guard contingent prepared for a German invasion in 1940 . . .

'When the invasion scare started, early in September, and we stood-to for a night and a day, the make-believe world of the Home Guard wore pretty thin. For my own lot were in position only three miles inland from the Seaton beaches and on the eastern flank of the Axe Valley, up which it was expected the enemy would thrust. We were scared that day, and if the Germans had landed, I dare say we should have been scattered like chaff; but we could see all round us what we should be fighting for – we were on our own doorsteps, after all – and we should have done our best; and I myself felt the full force and of life stripped down to essentials.'

One of my father's poems remembers this '*Stand To*' with something of a romantic glow. Another called '*Watching Post*' is in the same spirit:

A hill flank overlooking the Axe Valley.
Among the stubble a farmer and I keep watch
For whatever may come to injure our countryside –
Light-signals, parachutes, bombs, or sea invaders.
The moon looks over the hill's shoulders, and hope
Mans the old ramparts of an English night.

In a house down there was Marlborough born. One night
Monmouth marched to his ruin out of that valley
Beneath our castled hill, where Britons kept watch,
Is a church where the Drakes, old lords of this
countryside,
Sleep under their painted effigies. No invaders
Can dispute their legacy of toughness and hope.

Two counties away, over Bristol, the searchlights hope
To find what danger is in the air tonight.
Presently gunfire from Portland reaches our valley
Tapping like an ill-hung door in a draught. My watch
Says nearly twelve. All over the countryside
Moon-dazzled men are peering out for invaders.

The farmer and I talk for a while of invaders:
But soon we turn to crops – the annual hope,
Making of cider, prizes for ewes. Tonight
How many hearts along this war-mazed valley
Dream of a day when at peace they may work and watch
The small sufficient wonders of the countryside.

Image or fact, we both in the countryside
Have found our natural law, and until invaders
Come will answer its need: for both of us, hope
Means a harvest from small beginnings, who this night
While the moon sorts out into shadow and shape our
valley,
A farmer and a poet, are keeping watch.

July, 1940

However inadequate these men of the Home Guard were to defend
the country, and however badly equipped, they represented our
last chance. They were aware of it, of course, and their fearfulness
communicated itself to me. They were always expecting the order

to 'stand to', to get into position and await the Germans invading through Seaton. But the order never came again.

They weren't to know that it wouldn't. The prospect facing them all was a grim one, and much of their training was tedious, yet there was also a lot of fun to be had. There was clearly camaraderie among the men and among their wives too. The socials in Drakes Hall were always great occasions. The womenfolk would prepare the food. There was no shortage of that. They were good at inventing dishes and people generally grew a lot in their gardens to supplement what was produced on the farms. Raucous games like *Simple Simon Says* would be played and evacuees from London would generally lead the singing from the stage.

A stream of these evacuees was billeted on us during the early part of the war. One, a cockney lad called Reg Hogg – or Reg 'Og, as I have always remembered him because of the way he talked – stayed for quite a while. Later he was to return when the rockets started falling on London. Reg was two or three years older than me and probably a bad influence, teaching me things I shouldn't have known about at my age. He went to school in Axminster while I was sent by my parents to Allhallows at Rousdon. They probably hoped I wouldn't pick up the local accent, though it would have been better if I had. Instead I learned from Reg how to speak like a cockney. He went back to London before the end of the war, of course, and after two or three post-war visits I never heard from him again. I suppose my public school accent recovered over time.

At home I remember lying in bed as German planes droned overhead on their way to bomb Bristol or on their way back. They made a fearful throbbing noise, which my father in one of his poems called 'a cello drone'. Sometimes they would drop left-over bombs as they returned home. An incendiary landed in our garden at Musbury. It must have just missed our thatch: a lucky escape for us. Others were not as fortunate, for on another occasion, we watched from the garden as two planes came into the valley, turned just short of us and then, going back towards the sea, dropped bombs on a row of houses at Seaton. There was an enormous explosion and one house was destroyed. These, though, were isolated incidents. Exeter suffered so much worse. Friends of my parents came to stay with us when they were bombed out of the city. And from the cottage we could see a red sky when Bristol was on fire.

Despite my fear, I should probably have relished rather more enemy activity to report in my own newspaper. I never wanted to be anything other than a journalist, and one day, perhaps when I was 11 or 12 in the middle of the war, someone gave me an idea. A friend in Colyton who had also been bombed out of Exeter showed me his school newspaper. I knew straightaway that this was for me. For several years after that I produced my own. To start with, it was handwritten, but later my father gave me a typewriter. For the most part I reported on family affairs. We had cats we supposed were male and named them after war leaders, one of them General de Gaulle. We were wrong. On one subsequent issue, my splash headline was 'General has kittens'. Clearly I had a taste for a good story.

At the end of the war we climbed the hill to light a beacon. Half the village turned out. For some reason, the man who was the elder of the Plymouth Brethren, a man called Oscar Gear, made what was supposed to be the triumphal speech. As the church bells rang loud and clear from Colyton, he whined on about how he had seen the light 40 years before and about his experiences as a member of his church. I don't remember him saying a word about the end of the war, which we were meant to be celebrating.

My brother and I made every effort to mark victory with flags and the like, but curiously my parents were not inclined to rejoice. They said that the war had been a terrible thing to have happened and that so many people had died. In a way they were right, but few others restrained their own relief and joy.

The special edition of my own newspaper said it all. We had won.

Sean Day-Lewis became a journalist, reporting first for the Bridport News and later for a number of regional newspapers including the Wolverhampton Express and Star. In 1960 he joined the Daily Telegraph to write for the Peterborough gossip column. He became Fleet Street's first by-lined arts reporter and later the paper's TV and radio editor. When he retired in 1996 he had served the paper for 36 years. He has since written for Country Life from his home in Colyton.

Dennis Moss

Roaming the countryside on our bikes, we found the wreckage of a British fighter only a quarter of a mile from Colyton. Had it hit the town, the damage would have been huge

Across the field trailed a line of spilt petrol. Scratch marks scored the road, and to either side the hedges had been breached. Roots and branches lay tangled among the scattered earth, and the smell of cordite assaulted our senses.

We dropped our bicycles on the grass and ran towards what was left of the crashed German plane. Jagged pieces of the fuselage and wings were strewn over the field where it had come to violent rest.

My twin brother Alan and I may not have been the first witnesses that morning, 4 May 1942, to the plane's fate and we will certainly not have been the last. It must have been one of the most dramatic sights of war in the Colyton countryside.

A policeman stood guard over the wreckage, near Downhayne, not two miles from our home in Northleigh. An RAF airman hovered too. They didn't seem to mind the morbid curiosity of 13-year-old boys as we inspected the remains of a Junkers 88 that had crashed a few hours earlier, just before 3am.

An arm severed at the shoulder was all that connected this sprawl of metal with the men who the previous night had been aiming to fly back over the Channel. The gruesome find lay incongruously among the debris lying to one side of the cockpit.

The four crew of the aircraft, Unteroffiziers Hemmann, Kesselborn, Reps and Sars, had all perished in the crash. They had been shot down by a Beaufighter of RAF Squadron 307 crewed by two Polish airmen, Pilot Officer Lissowski and Sgt Illaszenicz.

Another day, roaming the countryside on our bikes, Alan and I excitedly found the wreckage of a British plane at Freakhayne Farm, near Southleigh. It had not long come down in the trees after the crew had baled out, apparently hoping it would ditch in the sea. In fact, it wasn't very far from Colyton. Had it hit the town, the damage would have been huge and people would almost certainly have died.

Part of the fighter was hanging in the branches of a tree. We walked around it, but soon left, just as the police arrived, because we could smell aviation fuel and feared an explosion.

These smashed planes, and their desperate crews intruding into our peaceful world below, were among the awful casualties of a war that seemed to pass us by.

All we would generally see and hear were German bombers throbbing to places whose destruction offered a greater incentive than our scattered farmhouses and villages. They would sometimes be chased, and maybe brought down, by RAF fighters determined to thwart them.

Later, we saw American Liberator planes criss-crossing the sky as they patrolled the Channel from Dunkeswell and towards the end of the war towed gliders on their way to the Arnhem landings.

Later still, as we stood by the cross at the bottom of the village, an American convoy passed us, picking its way inconspicuously through the narrow lanes, heading for the coast and eventually the Normandy beaches where so many of them would have died.

About 50 vehicles were crammed with high-spirited troops tossing out candy and chewing gum to anyone waving them farewell. They had been stationed at Wilmington, from where some had become regulars at the local pub. One called George, I remember, had sampled cider for the first time, from my father's barrel.

Earlier, the only incursion into our way of life had been by evacuees sharing our homes. For us, this had been quite literal.

We lived next to the village pub. It wasn't a big house, but our mother, a very kind lady, wanted to show all the hospitality she could to people fleeing the cities. So the Robinson family from London, mother and father and two girls under five, came to live with us.

The house was split down the middle. We used the front door; they used the back. They had a living room and a bedroom above; we had the other living room and bedrooms. I think they could cook on a range in their part of the house, and we had the kitchen. There was no bathroom, of course, just a tin bath, and we shared that. The toilet was 20 yards down the garden path.

It seems odd now that anyone would share their own home so completely with strangers, but, as kids do, we accepted it and got on with our lives. Our visitors stayed for about two years and then went back to London. We never heard from them again.

In every other way, life in the country went on much as before – except perhaps with a greater intensity. It had always been a struggle for ordinary country folk to make a living and feed their families. But now in wartime it was just a bit more difficult.

So we had all manner of schemes to put food on our plates and a little money in our pockets. If we bought a hundredweight of seed potatoes, the farmer would allow us a patch of land in which to plant them. He would look after them along with the rest of his crop, and at harvest-time we would collect the potatoes. With the farmer's permission, we would also pull up turnips from the fields. In return, the farmer would get our help at haymaking and harvest.

When the apples ripened in the orchards, we would pick them or collect them from the ground. We would get 6d a bag for those we knocked from the trees and 3d or 4d for those that had fallen. So now we had potatoes, turnips and apples to supplement all the vegetables and fruit we grew in our large garden.

In the fields were rabbits aplenty for the table and to sell to butchers. On Sunday mornings, sending a ferret down rabbit holes would yield 20 or 30, and for those we didn't eat ourselves we would get 2s a time.

Farmers would give you a penny for a mole's tail to be rid of the pests and Horace Friend, maker of coats and bags, would give you up to 2s for the skin. We caught thousands of them.

In father's carpentry shop, there were bits of wood he didn't want. We would split them up and make lighting sticks, tying them in bundles or bags such as you get from garages these days. They were worth a few pence each.

Gathering food or making money was much more fun than school. So from the age of 10 we would have two half-days a week out of the classroom. It was official; no truanting. The authorities would issue boys with a special card granting them permission to work on farms. And we would be paid by the farmer, too, for what we did. Not only did we get out of school, we were better off. I put this extra money into National Savings, and at 16 bought for £30 my first motor-bike, a 1935 Royal Enfield.

All this enterprise must have rubbed off from father. He did a bit of this and a bit of that, anything to earn a few bob.

He had several jobs, lending a hand wherever he could. By trade he was a carpenter, so he made coffins; and because he made coffins he was a pall-bearer at funerals; and because he was a pallbearer, he also dug graves.

He was a postman, too, and a part-time fireman, having fought the blaze in 1933 that damaged St Andrew's Church in Colyton, destroying the roof of the south aisle and a substantial part of the main nave. He was captain of the bellringers at the church, and he often accompanied the village bobby on night-time calls.

A true countryman for all seasons.

From 1943, Dennis Moss was apprenticed to Soanes Garage in Queen's Square, Colyton. In 1972 he took over the business, and in 1984 moved to a larger site near Green Bridge. In retirement, he continues to live in Colyton.

Muriel Turl

Years later, the soldier who had dug me out came back to find me. He wanted to make sure that what he had done had been worthwhile. We laughed and I thanked him

It was lunchtime in the big house. The major and his wife were finishing a light meal in the dining room, and I was making myself busy in the kitchen.

At the age of 14 I was in service, already getting used to working seven days a week, from early morning until the washing up was done after dinner in the evening.

Only weeks earlier, I had still been at school. Now I was a maid on a household staff of three, along with a cook and a cleaner. I even had to dress the part.

My employers were Major and Mrs Cartwright whose palatial home was on Seaton seafront. In the kitchen I had begun to clear away the pots and pans. It was late in 1942, on the 26th of October, a day like any other. Or so it had seemed.

Suddenly our world came to an end. A terrible explosion ripped through the house. In my fright I dashed into the hallway. I didn't know where I was going. For some reason I flung open the drawing room door and the blast caught me.

Four hours later they were digging me out of the rubble. I had been buried alive. Five people died at Seafield House that day, and I had been presumed the sixth. Searching for survivors, the rescuers' sound detectors had picked up nothing. Then a man from Beer heard me shout.

I had thought I was a goner. I was sure I would be suffocated. One of the men's shovels caught my outstretched arm locked in the rubble. I remember telling them to mind my hand or they would have it off.

There was an army of men trying to free me but a soldier appeared to be in charge. Eventually he lifted me clear of the fireplace that had pinned down my legs. One eye was out of its socket on my cheek, but apart from lacerations I was all right. They said the half-open door had saved me.

The soldier carried me to the Homestead nursing home along the seafront because there was no hospital in Seaton, and for a week or two the nurses there cared for me. Then they sent me home. I walked the mile or so back to Eyewell Green.

Whatever they did with the eye, they got it back again, though I have had a couple of operations on it since, and my back still bears the scars from that day. I was very lucky. Major Cartwright, who had retired from the army, and his wife were both killed, her body not found until the following day. Three others also died, including a young Wren who should have left the house that morning. Had she gone on time, she might still be alive. Apart from the Cartwrights, the dead were Miss Jill Wilkin, Miss Florence Sercombe and an elderly lady, Mrs Eleanor Ross.

Two others were luckier even than me. Neither the cook nor the cleaner had turned up for work that day.

Having been rescued so dramatically, I hit the papers a time or two. I felt quite like a celebrity. But the only times I had my picture taken were when I was carnival queen twice after the war.

I must have looked all right by then.

Years later, perhaps around 1970, the soldier who had dug me out came back to Seaton to find me. I was now working at Hayman's Dairy. He asked around until he discovered where I was working. I didn't recognise him because he looked quite an elderly man. He said he wouldn't have recognised me either. I suppose I looked much better than when he had last seen me. He joked that he wanted to make sure that what he had done had been worthwhile. We laughed about it and I thanked him. I don't know his name and I've never seen him again. But I owe him everything.

After all these years, the bomb from that Junkers 88 that might have killed me remains a horrible memory. Even now I can't bear water trickling down my face. I get flashbacks to being trapped in that house thinking blood was running from my head. It wasn't blood but dust and sand. Water feels just the same.

The house, of course, is no longer there. The stick of bombs that destroyed it had all landed on the house or in the garden at the back and blown the building apart. The house was never rebuilt. Where it had stood on the corner of Seahill and Castle Hill is now the site of the Jubilee Gardens. Behind stands the clock tower, whose time stuck resolutely at 1.20, as if offering a memorial to those killed by the bombs, until it was repaired some years later.

The bomber had come in from the sea, swung around and dived down to drop its deadly cargo, which blew out the windows and damaged roofs of buildings near the house. Wreckage was strewn around the streets. Its job done, the plane was lost to view as quickly as it had first been seen.

Yet, for all the drama of this terrible event, it merited just four paragraphs under the headline, 'House demolished, five killed', in the local newspaper, the *Pulman's Weekly News*. Censorship was strict then. The paper could only refer to Seaton as 'a small

South-West coast town'.

My job with the major and his wife had not lasted long and had ended tragically. It had been a brief glimpse into an age that was soon to pass. Few would live as my employers did, or work the long hours expected of me. The war changed everybody's lives.

Before the end of it all I registered to join the Wrens but by then I was working as a weaver for Gundry's, producing camouflage netting, and this was a reserved occupation. I didn't ever get to sample life in the forces.

After my adventure at the major's house, I learned to tell the difference between German planes and the RAF. You could tell the Germans by their drone. If I heard that noise, and the sirens went, I would bolt out of my parents' house. I wasn't going to be trapped again.

I would run up the lane and dive into a ditch beneath a hedge. And I would stay there until the all-clear. To this day I hate the sirens of police cars and ambulances.

Yet, for all the efforts of the German bomber who had frightened me so much, I lived to be married and to becoming a mother, grandmother and great-grandmother. I have a lot to be thankful for.

After the war, Muriel Hawker, left, the maid dug out of the bomber's rubble, married John Turl, a Colyton soldier. They made their first home in Seaton but later settled in Colyton. At different times Muriel worked as a caretaker at Colyton primary school and at the Colcombe Castle pub. Her husband was a postman for 30 years until his retirement in 1993.

Alan Board

Everyone was in a panic. We weren't at all prepared for invasion

I was working for this Exeter firm building a couple of pillboxes at Whitford and then we moved down into the mouth of the River Axe, where we started to build another. It was a stupid place they wanted it, in the gravel, on the beach.

Anyway, we were concreting the roof when a German plane came overhead and machine-gunned us. I saw the plane coming and just managed to dive off the pillbox on to the beach. The plane flew away and we climbed back up on to the roof and there we found spent cartridges. Our escape had been a narrow one.

We finished the pillbox, and then there was a storm. You can guess what happened. It tipped up, so we had to build another. And that one's still there.

They also had us building a sort of dam across the river with sandbags. The idea was to have a barrier against troop-carriers coming up the river. We almost got the two ends to meet in the middle when there was a high tide. All the sandbags were naturally washed down the river. Because of the tides, it was never going to work.

Everything was being done in a panic. We weren't at all prepared for a possible invasion.

Alan Board was 17 when war began and already at work on construction gangs. He was called up and served overseas. After being demobbed he returned to Colyton, where he worked as a builder. In retirement he continues to live in the town.

Frank Soanes

The stranger was suspected of being a German spy. Suddenly there was pandemonium. Hand grenades were primed with fuses and each man got five bullets

They hadn't expected such a dirty trick so we captured Seaton without ever confronting the enemy. It was all over before it had begun: game, set and match to Colyton Home Guard.

The manoeuvre had been planned by Captain Smith – Captain Mainwaring as he would have been in Dad's Army - and Lieutenant Percy Trivett. Very clever it was too.

They marched us to Colyton station, from where the trams now run, and put us all on the train, me on the footplate with the driver. We encountered no resistance because Seaton's Home Guard hadn't given a thought to the possibility that we might use the railway. Their defence had been to guard the roads.

While they manned their roadblocks, our train took us behind their lines and allowed us to take command of Seaton's town centre. We had such a laugh at their expense. Then as usual it was off to the pub.

We didn't have it all our own way, though. On another occasion, an exercise ended in embarrassing defeat on our own streets in Colyton.

A simulated attack came from the Special Services Home Guard. They were mainly fit and strong farmers who were trained better than us. In the event of a German invasion they were meant to act like commandos, causing as much havoc as possible. They would meet in secret dug-outs like the buried Nissen hut at Morganhayes and were held a little in awe by the ordinary Home Guard.

When they invaded the town we weren't sure what we were supposed to do. I took one look at the size of them and thought discretion the better part of valour. There wasn't any point in getting hurt for nothing. So we capitulated as shamefully as the Seaton men had done in the face of Captain Smith's and Lt Trivett's cunning ploy.

An earlier raid on Colyton by another Home Guard resulted in a thunderflash being thrown in the road outside my father's cycle shop on the corner of King Street and Church Street. It hardly scuffed the surface but shot grit at the shop's plate-glass window and shattered it. My father wasn't a bit happy.

At the time we lived over the shop. My father, a mechanic, had come from Oxford and bought the shop after the First World War. He also ran the garage next door and was to buy that later in the war.

I was following in my father's footsteps now I had left Colyton Grammar School. He had arranged my apprenticeship in Exeter, where I reported for my first day's work on 4 September 1939, the day after the war began. Every morning after that I caught an early train, once being delayed at Seaton Junction when a fast train came through taking French soldiers to Plymouth. They had been evacuated from Dunkirk and were being returned to the unoccupied western side of France.

When I joined Colyton's Home Guard in 1942 at the age of 18, it had about 40 men, some quite elderly, a few young like me and also farmers exempt from call-up. Because I was an apprentice engineer, I was also spared the forces, but by now we were all required to join the Home Guard. They met just over the road at Captain Smith's house, Colyton Cottage, and one night I wandered over and joined.

Some of the men had been involved since May 1940 when the Secretary of State for War, Anthony Eden, had appealed for units of Local Defence Volunteers to be formed to resist possible invasion by the Germans, who were then advancing rapidly through France and Belgium.

Retired regular army officers had formed a Seaton company with platoons at Colyton, Rousdon and Branscombe and had organised the recruitment of volunteers.

In the early days, the only weaponry was shotguns offered by the public. Ammunition was so scarce that shooting practice hadn't been possible. But by now, after a change of name to the Home Guard, guns and ammunition had become more generally available.

The first thing I needed as a new recruit was a private's uniform so I was taken by an old boy acting as the quartermaster to the Scout hut opposite The Grove in South Street and kitted out from the stock they kept there. It wasn't long before they gave me a rifle as well, but no ammunition. That was all kept at home by Captain Smith and issued only for shooting practice or an emergency.

There was only ever one of those and it came the day a stranger was seen in the area. It was suspected he might be a German spy. He was reported to the police and we were called out. Suddenly there was pandemonium over at Captain Smith's. Hand grenades, that we called Mills bombs, were all primed with fuses and each man was issued with five bullets. The enemy was thought to be

Platoons of the Home Guard; above, Colyton & below, Farway

in our midst so this was to be our big test. Yet before we had even reached the streets the emergency was declared a false alarm. The suspect had been identified as a hiker.

I don't know how many bullets we would have been allocated had the Germans invaded in strength but certainly five wouldn't have achieved much. Whatever I might have been given would have been made to count, though. For shooting was the one thing I could do well. I had been brought up on air guns and had always had a gun of some sort. We used to practise at a skittle alley in Colyford, where a small target was set up and we would shoot a 2.2 rifle at it. There would be 6d from everybody for the winner.

On Home Guard nights I would rush to catch the fast train from Exeter and then cycle from Seaton Junction. We would meet at St Andrew's Hall and form up for some drill and then be given training of one sort or another.

Every weekend we would do something. We would go into the countryside for an exercise or mount a guard overlooking the coast. We would act like soldiers even if we were playing at it, and it was all hugely enjoyable.

Sometimes we would go to Weston, near Sidmouth, where there were unprotected beaches, the sort of place it was feared the Germans might choose for a landing. Some would patrol down on the beach while others remained on the cliffs above to keep a look-out, though more than likely they would be in a hut there smoking and playing cards.

At Weston we would occasionally practise with a rifle that had a grenade fixed to the end of its barrel. I don't remember what they were called but the idea was to have a mobile form of artillery. We fired them down in the goyle there.

These were about the only shots we fired out in the field, though occasionally we went to a rifle range near Bonehayne Farm, not

Frank Soanes, right, with Colyton hairdresser Ted Long who was at home on leave from the RAF

far from Colyton. There we would shoot at targets sunk into the side of a hill. It had been used by Colyton volunteers before the First World War, and more recently by the police and Allhallows School cadets.

To see real action we would sometimes go to the White Hart at Colyford and buy some cheap Empire wine, then walk to Boshill Cross, near Axmouth. From there, between tipples, we could watch the frequent German raids on Portland to the east.

From March 1944, as the Allied invasion of Europe was being prepared, responsibility for Britain's defence fell to the Home Guard. I had gone to work as an engineer in Bristol so I missed the greater intensity of beach patrols that followed until the D-Day landings had been secured. In December, it was all over for us. We were disbanded because an invasion threat no longer existed. After final parades we handed in everything but our uniforms and boots. I dyed my khaki greatcoat dark blue. It was always lovely and warm.

In truth we had not been needed. Our training had been for an invasion that thankfully never came. Capturing Seaton by train had been our moment of glory.

Had the Germans landed on one of the local beaches we would have been Britain's last line of defence, and doing our best would have counted for little.

But it had all been fun and it had kept up people's morale, even if that was only our own.

As the war ended, Frank Soanes was working as an engineer in Bristol. He returned to Colyton and at the age of 26 took over his father's business in 1949. Many years later he rented the garage to an employee and went to work in Exeter while his wife continued to run the cycle shop. His son later managed the shop, which has now been sold. In his retirement Frank Soanes continues to live in Colyton.

Germans who disturbed the peace

Its unlikely graveyard was tiny Eight Shillings field. The mighty plane was burned out. Nothing survived but a bomb that lay unexploded in a shallow crater.

White cloud obscured the German bomber from the ground, so its vulnerability to attack from a fighter of the resurgent RAF was from above.

Realising that his aircraft would be silhouetted against the moonlit cloud beneath, the pilot, Oberleutnant Kurt Gumbart, at 29 the oldest of the crew of four, instructed his wireless/telegraph operator, Willi Zastrau, to keep a sharp look-out overhead.

Vigilantly, he had kept changing his aircraft's course and varying its height between a maximum of 6,500ft and a minimum of 3,500ft as it flew over East Devon, but because it was now nearing its target it was flying a straight course.

Its mission was to rain destruction on Exeter, a city reckoned to be the second most impressive architectural site in the south after Bath. Exeter had no strategic significance. It had been selected in revenge for the Allied bombing of Lubeck, and this was to be the first of many raids it would suffer, the worst coming the following month.

Kurt Gumbart's bomber had a payload of two 1,400kg bombs, all it could carry on a five-hour round trip without an intermediate landing in France.

Stalking the same skies that dark night in 1942 were Pilot Flying Officer Thorp and his wireless operator, Sergeant King, in their Beaufighter, of RAF 604 squadron, Middle Wallop. They were on the look-out, too – for enemy bombers like Gumbart's.

What they saw from over the sea interested them. As the Germans had predicted, the target they spotted lay below them. They caught sight of the enemy aircraft again soon afterwards, and then lost it among the cloud for 10 minutes. Now crucially it was above them. They increased speed and climbed but had to throttle back because their target was flying more slowly, now on a straight and level course to the west.

With the moon in F/O Thorp's eyes, they saw the silhouette of the enemy plane again. They closed in from below and recognised it as a Dornier 217. Having identified it, they drew back and opened fire from between 50 and 100 yards and from a slightly lower level. From their cannon, 51 rounds were shot at the bomber.

Almost instantaneously, flames poured from the Dornier's port engine. Thorp banked his fighter to the right and then swung back to watch the bomber, now enveloped by flame along the whole length of its fuselage, dive vertically to its doom. It passed through cloud beneath its attacker and lit up the sky with a brilliant flash as it exploded.

Two shots had hit the tail of the plane and others pierced the fuselage, one severely injuring engineer Lothar Barthel's hand. Fatefully, most of the shots had holed the fuel tank.

Later, pilot Gumbart was to inform intelligence officers that the engine was still running but that the tank was blazing like a torch. He gave the order to bale out and soon afterwards baled out himself.

It was 11.25pm on 23 April. A patrolling aircraft reported the crash happening 15 miles east of Exeter. The mighty plane had actually come down on a tiny, triangular piece of land immediately to the east of the railway embankment carrying the line from Seaton Junction to Exeter and almost opposite a Nissen hut, which was

The next day at Eight Shillings field, Umborne, as RAF and bomb disposal officers tackle unexploded bombs and crash debris

the site of a searchlight.

Its unlikely graveyard was Eight Shillings field near the hamlet of Umborne, part of the parish of Shute. It was burned out. Almost nothing survived except one of its bombs, which lay unexploded in a shallow crater among small pieces of debris. The other bomb fell on a nearby hillside.

Willi Zastrau, aged 26, and observer Rudolf Zimmerhackel and Barthel, both 25, baled out in quick succession some time before Kurt Gumbart. They landed in Northleigh, one at Chilcombe Farm, a second in a tree on the edge of Bucknole Farm and a third at Combe Farm.

At Chilcombe, Zastrau came to ground among cows, which gathered around him in the dark. He was frightened. His cries in German could be heard across the valley. Bill Baily, a special constable, had already been alerted to the drama. A plane with engine trouble had been heard overhead and then a red glow had been seen in the distance as it crashed.

'You've got to come with me,' Baily had said to thatcher Gordon Snell, a member of the Home Guard, and to Jack Batten, a farmer. In his lorry, they went to investigate. They rescued the frantic German from the inquisitive cows and drove off towards the village police house.

Barthel, the injured engineer, and Zimmerhackel were close to each other as they came down to earth, close enough for the pained Barthel to be heard calling out: 'Rudolf, Rudolf'. Zimmerhackel had first to extricate himself from the tree. He knocked on the door at Combe Farm, where Bill Matthews was looking out of the window. Farmer Matthews saw Zimmerhackel bury his revolver in a culvert. The German was soon to be picked up by Bill Baily's lorry.

At much the same time, Mrs Biddick was on her way home in

Northleigh after a visit to her father nearby. As she turned towards her front door, she had the fright of her life. Sheltering in her porch was the injured airman. He had not wanted to alarm her, but of course he did.

The war had come a little too close for Mrs Biddick's comfort. But all Barthel wanted was her help. She lived only two or three doors from the policeman's house, where the three German air crew were soon to be reunited. PC Ernest Pester was out, already called to the crashed plane. But, in time-honoured English custom, his wife served tea to her unexpected guests.

Gumbart was later to describe his own landing: 'Suddenly I saw my parachute above me, but I saw nothing more of the aircraft. Then I landed, jarred my spine a bit and sprained my thumbs. There was a farmhouse some 50 metres away. I went towards it. First I had to crawl through a hedge, after leaving my parachute lying on the ground.

'The rest of my crew had long since disappeared. They had baled out perhaps half a minute before me. I went up to the house, shouted, but got no answer.'

That house was Higher Watchcombe Farm. Inside asleep were an evacuee from London, Denis Swann, and a Land Army girl from Wales, May Summers.

The airman wandered down the lane and knocked on the door of Lower Watchcombe Farm. The door was answered by Barbara Gear, to whom Gumbart spoke in English, though it was obvious from his uniform and his accent that he was German. Frightened, she called out to her uncle, Charlie Gear, a prisoner of the Germans during the First World War. He wanted his rifle to shoot their unwelcome visitor.

Gumbart lay down his pistol to demonstrate he was surrendering as Barbara ran out of the house through a back door and down the field to Little Parkhayne, where Jack Train lived. Mr Train was the first lieutenant in the local Home Guard. He had seen the plane in flames in the valley below and came straightaway.

He called Johnny Clarke from Halsehayne, another member of the Home Guard, and together they arrested Gumbart, who is said to have told his captors that he could speak English because he had been to college in Exeter.

Gumbart was then taken to Higher Watchcombe to await transport to Honiton. By now, evacuee Denis Swann was awake and sitting by the fireside in the kitchen. He watched as the group of men came into the room, the German in his flying leathers. The pilot was told to sit at the long table, where he was given a supper of bread and cheese and a glass of cider.

Later, as he was marched out to a waiting vehicle, he showed his appreciation for the way he had been treated by taking off his coat and, with his flying gloves, giving it to May Summers.

Though she could hardly stand in the coat because of its weight, she was to treasure her unlikely gifts for the rest of her time at Higher Watchcombe.

Gumbart, Zimmerhackel, Zastrau and Barthel were all taken to Honiton police station. There, Dr Hoffman, whose own family background was German, was called to examine Barthel's wound. He found the German's hand hanging from his arm by a sinew. All he could do was cut it off and dress the wound. He is said to have thrown the severed hand on to the fire before sending Barthel to the Royal Devon and Exeter Hospital.

By daybreak, work to clear the wreckage of their plane from Eight Shillings field was beginning. Nothing of any importance to intelligence officers was to be salvaged.

A bomb disposal squad, led by Squadron Leader Hubert

Dinwoodie, was on its way and soon the site would be returned to the spring's fast-growing grass and wild flowers, occasionally giving up fragments of buried metal to local souvenir hunters.

Many years later, papers in the National Archives marked 'Most Secret' revealed that Gumbart and Zastrau had been recorded in extraordinary exchanges with other German airmen, one a fighter pilot captured seven weeks earlier and the other a bomber pilot detained a week after the Shute crash. These recordings had been made at an interrogation unit in London where all Luftwaffe personnel were questioned before being sent to prisoner-of-war camps.

Zastrau, who seemed more concerned about how in his absence his wife would obtain his precious Dutch purchases of fine things to eat and drink including nine bottles of liqueur, 12lbs of chocolate and a range of hard-to-get groceries, described the Dornier's last moments.

'We were flying straight because we were just approaching the target and had to stay on our course.'

Zastrau spoke of another German plane that was subsequently shot down and reported what its wireless operator had said. 'He saw the enemy aircraft about two kilometres in front of him against a cloud. It flew lower and then suddenly zoomed, and he saw it just above him. Then he noticed that it was changing course. At that moment he (the British fighter) fired and was about 20 metres from the aircraft.

'I tell you I could see the flames from the exhaust. I recognised it at once. ''That's a Beaufighter,'' I said.

'I could see nothing but flames in front and then I thought we must have got a hit in the port engine. I looked and it was going s-s-s-h. It was burning already. It all happened in a second or two; it was all so quick.'

The next morning, as unexploded bombs were being defused at Umborne, farmer Edgar Hurford went to attend to his sheep. There, among them, he found what had landed with such a thud in the previous night's darkness. An airman's boot.

One of the Germans had left without a hand, another without a boot.

Evacuee Denis Swann with Land Army Girl May Summers outside Higher Watchcombe

Alan Copp

'Out of the line of fire', he kept shouting. It was all very comical

We were out rabbiting at Combe Gulley at the top of what was then West Street in September 1940 when the church bells rang. That was only supposed to happen if there was an invasion.

We scurried up to the top where you can see right over Seaton and the sea, but there didn't appear to be anything happening. So we carried on rabbiting until about 10pm. It was double summertime then and so it remained light until later. And then we came back to Colyton, down West Street, now The Butts.

When we got to the narrow bit of Sidmouth Road just below Copp's, the blacksmith's shop, there were carts and other obstructions across the road. The Local Defence Volunteers or Home Guard, whichever it was at the time, wouldn't let Tom Davey and me through, though, of course, they knew who we were. They sat on their shotguns and said they were under orders not to allow anyone into town. Oh well, I said, we'll go up School Lane and climb over the walls and get into the bakery from there. That's what we'll do. Then they decided they would let us through.

Everybody was opening their doors and trying to make out what was going on as the men paraded up and down. And as they did, Colonel Dixon, who was in charge, was shouting down the street at the top of his voice, 'Out of the line of fire', 'Out of the line of fire'. It was all very comical.

Alan Copp was 13 at the time. His family had run Copps bakery from 1922 and he would soon take charge. He retired in 1989 and later the business closed. Alan still lives in Colyton.

Colyton's St John Ambulance brigade on parade before the town's people

Women at work at the 'secret' munitions factory at Branscombe

Doris Sanders

Surprisingly perhaps, Colyton had four bakers' shops. There were four butchers. In all, there were 40 shops in Colyton. They helped to make the town self-sufficient

For 2d a time they were having their Sunday roasts cooked at the baker's. They would stream by our cottage window, baking tins in hand, each with a joint of meat and potatoes ready for the oven.

Taking a break from my own chores, I would watch this curious little procession passing up Queen Street to Copps, the largest of Colyton's bakers.

Having delivered their meat raw to the baker, they would stroll on to church and later call for their dinners as they returned home. It would be 12.45 now and steam would be rising from beneath the white cloth that covered their tins of piping-hot food as they hurried back down Queen Street.

The arrangement suited both the baker and his customers. Copps didn't bake on Sundays but didn't want, either, to lose heat from their ovens, so cooking people's dinners gave them some return on the coke banked up as usual the previous evening. Many of their customers with large families and small cooking ranges didn't have ovens big enough for joints and poultry, so they got the main meal of the week cooked for them. As many as 30 or 40

The Copp family outside their baker's shop in Queen Street

used the service.

It was the same at Christmas. People would queue with their baking tins, this time charged perhaps with a goose: festive dinners ready for the oven at Copps the bakers.

The practice had been followed for years, and now as a 15-year-old I was watching it stretch into wartime.

In the cities, where meat was scarcer, they would hardly have believed it, even at the time. But here there weren't the same shortages. People ate simply during the week; rabbits, for example, were plentiful and provided a good stew. Rationing coupons would be saved for the feast on Sundays. It was the highlight of the week.

Next day, Copps would open again, shelves laden now with bread, white and brown, baked from 4 am. On different days of the week, the usual cakes and pastries prepared the previous afternoon would be supplemented with something special, like cream buns on Fridays, which sometimes we would have for a treat.

Surprisingly perhaps, Colyton had four bakers' shops. As well as Copps, there was Govers in Dolphin Street, where the Bakehouse bistro is now, Bastables in Vicarage Street, where I would buy a bag of broken biscuits for 2d, and the Co-op, on the site of the CeramTec factory in Sidmouth Road.

The bigger shops had delivery rounds in town and around the villages. Through the war, the Copp family, who had served the Colyton area since 1922 and would go on doing so until 1989, continued to use a horse and cart for their town round. A Model 'T' Ford van now supplied the villages, some of them daily and others farther away three times a week.

Service to the doorstep survived through the war and in some cases beyond. Milk from the farms and dairies lasted longest as a delivered commodity. But bread, groceries, meat and fish all came to people's doors if they wanted it – and often even those in the same streets as the shops took a delivery.

In all, there were about 40 shops for Colyton's 2,000 people, and some doubled up to cater separately for men and women or served more than one purpose. They all helped to make the town self-sufficient.

People would buy their commodities and clothing in specialist, individual shops rather than one-stop shopping at supermarkets and department stores that proliferate now.

There were four butchers: Loud's in the Market Place, White's next to the Gerrard Arms in St Andrew's Square and Harris's on the corner of Market Place. For a while there was also Rendall's in Queen's Square.

Grocers, too, provided lots of choice. There were seven of them, all offering something a little different from the next. Mills's in Dolphin Street was a place to go for everyday bits and pieces. Trumps, at the top of Queen Street, were high-class grocers, like the shop still bearing the name in Sidmouth. In the Market Place, White's and Follett's vied for people's custom. White's, where the Spar shop is now, would sell lovely ice cream in summer, and at the bigger Follett's shop, wrapping around the corner and including Wilkies and the hairdressers of today, two chairs would be positioned at the counter where you could wait in comfort as assistants made up your order.

At the dairy shop in King Street, Mr Thorn sold everything from milk, cheese and eggs to home-made pasties and cream doughnuts. He also supplied milk in one-third pint bottles to the school. Volunteers to return the empties were always available because they would usually be rewarded with a doughnut or bun.

And there were at least as many sweet shops, here a farthing's worth for children, there high-class confectionery and even home-made treats. At Brokenshires near the Lloyds bank, you might buy chocolates or other delicacies. The shopkeeper there was also the choirmaster at St Andrews, and he gave private lessons on the violin and piano. By contrast, only a few yards away at the corner of Hillhead, Mr Wood sold cheap sweets among the dogs and rabbits he also kept. We were forbidden from going there for fear of what we might be eating, but if we could get away with it we would defy mum's instructions because you got more for your money. Somehow they all survived, at least through the war, probably because of all the evacuees and billeted soldiers and the larger families of the time. Until the war, it was usual to have six children or more. Only a family of 14 or 15 was considered exceptional.

There were tobacconists, drapers and haberdashers, men's and ladies' clothing stores, and shoe shops and repairers. There was wallpaper and paint in one shop, toys and books in another. There were watches and clocks, saddlery and animal feedstuffs. And as now, there was a bank, a post office and a chemist's; hairdressers, cycles and a garage, hardware and fish and chips. Oh yes, and there was also the tannery, which would sell you a piece of leather to mend your boots or shoes.

Mrs Harvey, the haberdasher on Queen's Square (later to be a butcher's shop), had cottons and ribbons and would ride her bike out into the country to sell her goods. Her husband had a fish and chip shop across the passageway from her own and was also a so-called 'walking postman'. Like one or two other traders, he walked a country route for the Post Office at a slack time of day.

Symons was the place to go for your Sunday best. It was a large shop occupying London House, where the charity and book shops are now in Market Place. Ladies' fashions were in one area, menswear in another. Upstairs were children's clothes and hats. Around the corner in Vicarage Street were shoes. When you made your purchase, the money and invoice would be put into a pneumatic tube and fired along the wire at ceiling height to the cashier. A bell would ring when your change and a receipt came hurtling back the same way to the counter.

If your new clothes needed alteration, they could be delivered later to your home by an errand boy on the shop bike, even if you lived in villages as far away as Southleigh or Whitford.

The best fun to be had from Colyton's shops was watching the men trimming the wallpaper in Hoopers, who were painters and decorators near what is now the Kingfisher pub. Then wallpaper came from the manufacturers with a blank edging and the shop had a special machine to strip it away. The paper used to go everywhere.

But the most pleasure came in the form of a bike from Soanes. Paying for it on the 'never, never' had a reverse meaning in those days. I had to wait interminably for my new pride and joy. For, rather than riding away on the bike and paying in instalments afterwards, I saved for it week by week until my card was fully stamped. Then the bike was mine.

In addition to all this business activity, Colyton had its own railway station, connecting the town from its very doorstep to the national rail network. You could go anywhere you wanted and anyone could reach you, as the influx of evacuees and soldiers proved very well.

The town also had its own electricity supply, which many of its people were reluctant to give up after nationalisation, its own gas and its own water. It had its own coal merchant, too, Mark Strawbridge, whose neighbour at the bottom of Dolphin Street, Mr Harris, was the parcels carrier, collecting packages from the station with his horse and wagon and delivering them around the town.

Six pubs – there had been eight – met wartime drinkers' needs. In addition to today's pubs, the Gerrard Arms, the Kingfisher (then called the Globe) and the Colcombe Castle, the Bear stood at Chantry Bridge, the Country House Inn in Sidmouth Road and the White Hart in Church Street.

The Compasses at the top of South Street had been the last pre-war closure and was now yet another sweet shop catering for what seemed like hundreds of children at a farthing, ha'penny or penny a time.

Within reason, you could get anything you wanted in Colyton, which was just as well because most people travelled hardly anywhere else. Most of them didn't have cars, though by the outbreak of war a few vehicles had replaced the clatter of horses' hooves on the streets. For the most part, if you couldn't walk or cycle, you didn't go. A trip by train was special, though some used it for commuting to Seaton or Exeter. People generally lived their lives where they were, taking a delivery of this or shopping for a little of that.

Colyton was a very different place from now, a proper town, where all people's daily needs were satisfied, rather than the village it resembles today.

Doris Sanders, left, was a Land Army girl in Herefordshire during the war, and afterwards worked for a year at Colcombe Mill Farm, back in Colyton. In 1949, she went to Australia, married there and had two children. She worked for an agricultural college and a dairy association before returning again to Colyton in 1972 after her husband's death.

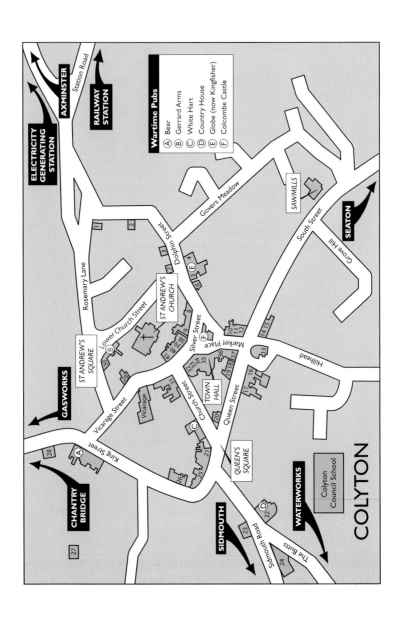

COLYTON

Wartime Pubs
- (A) Bear
- (B) Gerrard Arms
- (C) White Hart
- (D) Country House
- (E) Globe (now Kingfisher)
- (F) Colcombe Castle

ELECTRICITY GENERATING STATION

AXMINSTER

Station Road

RAILWAY STATION

Govers Meadow

Dolphin Street

SAWMILLS

South Street

Grove Hill

SEATON

Rosemary Lane

Lower Church Street

ST ANDREW'S CHURCH

ST ANDREW'S SQUARE

GASWORKS

Vicarage Street

Vicarage

Silver Street

Market Place

Church Street

TOWN HALL

Queen Street

Hillhead

King Street

CHANTRY BRIDGE

QUEEN'S SQUARE

SIDMOUTH

Sidmouth Road

The Butts

WATERWORKS

Colyton Council School

COLYTON

Map references

Shops and businesses are shown in the positions they occupied in Colyton at the outbreak of war, when many of the streets had different names. To avoid confusion, they are superimposed on streets as they are today. The numbers on the map accord with the list below:

1 Harris, parcels carrier

2 Strawbridge, coal merchant

3 Holmwood, confectionery

4 Mills, grocer

5 Turl, shoemaker

6 Hooper, paint/wallpaper

7 Gover, baker

8 Hoyle, grocer

9 Davis, saddler

10 Woodgate, draper

11 Brokenshire, confectionery

12 Matthews, hairdresser

13 Jacknall, cobbler

14 Wood, basketmaker

15 Johnson, confectionery

16 Trumps, grocer

17 Copp, baker

18 Abraham, confectionery

19 Hoare, fishmonger/greengrocer

20 Harvey, haberdashery

21 Soanes, cycles/garage

22 Copp, blacksmith

23 Co-op, grocer/baker

24 Cooper, confectionery

25 Long, hairdresser/ newsagent/ tobacconist

26 Thorn, dairy products

27 Baker, tannery

28 Turl, blacksmith

29 Bastable, baker/grocer

30 White, butcher

31 Symons, ladies and gents outfitter/shoes

32 Smith, newsagent/toys/lending library

33 Loud, butcher

34 Post office/telephone exchange

35 Follett, grocer/ironmonger

36 White, grocer/shoes

37 Harris, butcher

38 David, later Towse, chemist

39 Ayres, clock repairer/jeweller

40 Follett store

41 Pearce/Wiseman, grocer

Gordon White

One and half ounces of cheese per person, per week, two ounces of sugar, four ounces of bacon, stipulated amounts of lard, margarine and tea. You couldn't be a fraction out

I hurried home. School had finished at four o'clock and by a quarter past I was expected to be in father's shop, apron tied around my waist, serving customers. As I ran along Church Street, through Colyton, I knew that if I were as little as five minutes late, I would be in trouble.

Other children might be allowed to play out with their friends before tea, but my place was in the family grocer's shop my father ran next to the town hall in Market Place, where the Spar shop is now.

His word was law. From the age of 10 that meant my being at work when I wasn't at school, six days a week and Sunday morning. If I wasn't serving at the counter, I would be delivering orders, and if I wasn't delivering orders, I would be cleaning the floors.

Scrubbing the shop floor was a Monday morning job before school. I would be down on my hands and knees, lifting out last week's grime before the new week began. Then I would lay newspaper to soak up what remained of the soap and water before the first customers arrived.

I didn't mind. I didn't know any other way of life. The shop was at the centre of everything we did, even after lunch on Sunday afternoon, supposedly our only free time. But that's another story, and I'll come to that.

As war broke out I was 11 and learning the trade that was always to occupy me. Three years later I would leave school and go into the shop full time.

Long before then I could bone a side of bacon in no time at all. I would wrap it in greaseproof paper, in one-ounce, two-ounce and four-ounce packs. Whatever amount of cheese the customer could have, she got, sliced from the big block on the board using a cheese wire. I would pat butter into neat rectangular shapes and wrap it expertly.

Along with almost everything else, sugar was loose. I would pour it into blue bags, weigh it accurately, tilt the pack and fold down the top so none of the precious white crystals escaped.

All the time, my father would hover in the background, making sure every customer was treated properly and that she got exactly what she asked for and exactly what her coupon book allowed. He was a stickler for getting everything just right: one and half ounces of cheese per person, per week, two ounces of sugar, four ounces of bacon, stipulated amounts of lard, margarine and tea. You couldn't be a fraction out. Father made sure we understood that the tiniest discrepancy one way was unfair to the customer, and unlawful, and the other way costly to us. People were entitled to precise weights and that's what they paid for.

Tearing out coupons from customers' books as they bought their groceries was a constant reminder of war, though little else prompted us to think of other people's sufferings. News on the radio sometimes made us realise how lucky we were, and a visit to Exeter with my father certainly did.

He had sent a radiogram for repair in the city before the bombing started. Then the blitz came. My father wanted to know what had happened to his radiogram, so off we went in his car. Even on the outskirts, you couldn't describe what you were seeing. It was like being driven into a different world. Buildings were smouldering. People were wandering aimlessly. Fire engines were everywhere, and ambulances too. There was a quietness that you didn't associate with a city. It was like everything had been switched off. I've never forgotten that. We were trying to get to the main street, to the radio shop on the left-hand side going down the hill. And, amid the devastation, no building was recognisable except the cathedral, and that was stood up straight as if it was all-powerful in the rubble.

In all, 265 people died in Exeter's air raids, apparently undertaken by Hitler in revenge for the bombing of the cathedral city of Lubeck. More than 1,500 houses and 400 shops were flattened.

The mere fact of our going to Exeter for such a trivial purpose pointed up the difference between life in the city and life at home. Back in Colyton, Mr Jenkins, our schoolteacher, had us practising again taking shelter from the enemy. Under his instructions, we had cleared the ditch beneath a hedge running up the hill from the school. Now Mr Jenkins was blowing his whistle again and we were standing in line at the front of the classroom ready to be marched out to hide under the hedge. We never had to do it for real.

After school it was back in the shop, behind the mahogany counter and beside the polished till, scales and bacon slicer. Behind were the shelves on which tins and packets were displayed and at a lower level the big drawers that pulled out to reveal the loose foods that had to be weighed out and packed on demand for customers. At six o'clock, mother would call us to the table for tea, interrupted often by a bell telling us that someone needed serving in the shop. We would stay open until eight or nine in the evening.

Finally we closed for the week at Sunday lunchtime. Then afterwards came the wartime ritual of sorting people's ration coupons. These were spread out on the dining table cleared now of plates and cutlery. While mother washed up in the kitchen, the counted coupons were threaded in 50s or 100s on to little pieces of cardboard in their separate colours, buff for this, pink for that, green for the other.

Once a month, these curious clutches of coloured paper were taken to the Ministry of Food offices in Axminster and exchanged for the next month's allocation of commodities. Whatever you had sold one month would be allowed you the next. A hundredweight of sugar one month would be followed by a hundredweight, and so on. In this way, shopkeepers were rationed according to the rations of their customers.

Outside this rigid system there was the black market, food from under the counter that the ministry knew nothing about. Some shops probably operated it, but not father. He thought it unjust because it meant some customers being favoured over others. He wouldn't have tolerated that at all. In some ways he might have been a bit of a tyrant, but he set a good example to his children. You might say we worked hard but we were brought up well.

There was fun to be had too. I went to the youth club in Church Street. Opposite lived a lady who shouted at us when we laughed and made a noise in the street. When the dark nights came we would get our revenge. We rigged up a contraption that knocked her door when, out of sight, we pulled a string. Time and again she would come to the door, find nobody there and turn on her heels swearing at those damned boys.

Then there was the competition among us to see who could record the most German planes flying overhead intent on injury and damage to people far away.

And, best of all, there were the Americans who for a period lived next door to us in Bath House. They were a great bunch. One huge fellow called Wayne Parker had the room looking into my bedroom window. Over the passageway we would chat for what seemed like hours.

They would allow us into the dances in the town hall. We were fascinated. We had never seen anything like it. Jitter-bugging, they called it. We couldn't believe it would ever catch on in our country.

How wrong we were.

Gordon White worked in his father's business until he was 25. He became a sales rep in the grocery trade, working first in the Dunstable area and then in Torquay. He managed holiday flats for a while and later retired to Colyford.

Barbara Dean

My grandfather had brought electricity to Colyton in the years before the war. So there was the generating station still to run and people's accumulators to charge

The siren wailed in Colyton and my mother and I hurried along Dolphin Street towards the water culvert we used as a shelter when an air raid threatened.

We didn't make it in time. A German fighter swooped low and his gunfire crackled in the still air. I can't be sure the pilot was aiming at us. I can't even say that I was very frightened. What I do remember is seeing the silhouette of a figure in the cockpit and being mesmerised by him.

It was as if the pilot had come from another world and had entered mine, and then he was gone.

Perhaps I was too young to understand how nearly we might have perished. I don't think we children were very conscious of the seriousness of the war, however exciting at times it seemed to be. I was, after all, only seven when it all started.

Sometimes we would hear the droning of engines overhead as German bombers headed for Bristol or Cardiff using the River Exe and Axe as markers. After bombarding one of the cities they would drop their remaining incendiaries near the coast. Seaton had plenty, and some fell behind where I lived, Colcombe Mills Farm, on the Whitford road.

We heard from the radio about what was going on, but the enormity of it all didn't really register. It wasn't until later when you saw what damage had been done in places like Exeter and Plymouth that you really understood how some people had suffered.

By the time of the big raid on Exeter in 1942, my father had rented out the farm and been employed by the Ministry of Supply. He had been put in charge of all the sawmills producing timber from Wimborne to Penzance. After the bombing, it took him half a day to get across Exeter to collect wages for the men. He came back with a terrible story.

In Colyton life went on pretty much the same as it had always done, though the town was blacked out after dark. We had dyed sheets behind the curtains so that light didn't leak out of windows and alert enemy aircraft to our whereabouts. If any light was showing outside, patrolling wardens would bang on the door and tell you to put it out.

My grandfather Frederick Hann had brought electricity to Colyton in the years before the war. So there was the generating station still to run and there were people's accumulators to charge.

The Petters and Rushton generators ran all day at the farm but were switched off at night so that their noise did not disturb anyone. Then charged batteries took over until early the next day when the generators were turned on again.

People used accumulators to power their radios. When these needed recharging, Grandma Mabel would collect them in her little car from houses around the town and nearby countryside, take them home and do the job in the battery house, which had been part of the old stable block. She would then load them up and drive them out again, all for 6d a time.

Grandfather had started by installing power at his own home, Coly House, in Rosemary Lane, and then connecting his neighbours. By the outbreak of war, most people had electricity from my grandfather's company, Colyton Electric Light and Power Supply. The streets were lit, too.

The company was one of the last surviving private supply companies. It had been one of more than 600 such companies around the country. Most were absorbed by the new nationalised industry after 1948 but grandfather stayed in business for another two years. It was only then that mains power came to Colyton. I still have some of the old company notepaper but now it bears nothing more than some of my recipes.

Father did a milk round. At first it was with a pony and cart, and the milk came to people's houses in churns. He would measure out pints into people's jugs outside their doors. Later he used an old Ford van and my mother helped him. It was quite a job because he would deliver twice a day. He said that his customers wanted half a pint in the morning and half a pint in the afternoon so that it was always fresh. Why they couldn't have had a pint in the morning, I don't know.

Living on a farm, we always had plenty of food, unlike less fortunate people in the cities. I don't think farming families went short of anything, and when you needed more they would be so generous. After Dunkirk we had 18 soldiers billeted on the farm for some weeks. Though the army provided rations for them, people wanted them to have more. We had food of our own we would share with them but other people would come to the door and leave great sacks of vegetables, rabbits, pheasants, anything they had. They said it was the least they could do for 'our boys'.

The soldiers had their own cook. Alfred was his name, and he couldn't boil water. When there was cooking to be done, mother would shout: 'Where's old Alfred?' He would be found swinging to and fro on my swing hanging from the apple tree. So my mother would get on with the cooking herself.

There were lots of other soldiers billeted on Colyton from time to time. They were seldom any trouble, though once I remember my gold watch being stolen from the kitchen dresser. I don't know who had it but I never saw it again. I couldn't understand how anyone would want to steal a little girl's watch.

People got to know some of the soldiers. My father liked one of the Czechs billeted at The Grove in Cuckoo Street. He lent him his violin so the soldier could play the music he loved. A year after the war ended I went to the World Youth Festival in Prague and was able to look him up. That was quite an experience travelling across Europe and seeing what the war had done to various countries. By then, nothing had been rebuilt, of course. There was devastation everywhere, much of it caused by ourselves as we freed the continent from Germany's tyranny.

Near Prague, I attended a memorial service for inhabitants of Lidice massacred by the Germans in revenge for the killing of the deputy head of the Gestapo, Reinhard Heydrich. Altogether, 191 men and boys over 16 had been shot in 1942. Seven women had been shot and 195 sent to a concentration camp. Ninety children had been distributed according to race around German families, who were to bring them up as their own. The village had been burned to the ground.

The open-air service was so moving. It made me realise how horribly people had suffered while we in Colyton had been virtually untouched by six years of war.

After the Czechs in Colyton came Poles and then Americans. The locals didn't seem to mind all their wartime guests. I suppose they felt sorry for young men far from home. Everyone was so friendly. The Americans, of course, had more than anyone else and would love to give sweets and gum to the children.

One of my strangest experiences - though nobody would think it the least strange now -was when we children were out in the fields looking for the first primroses of the new season. We were at the top of Hillhead, and a US army lorry went by. Its canvas came up at the back and there was this great black face.

This was 60 years ago, mind you. We had never seen a black man before.

Barbara Dean finished her education at Colyton Grammar and trained as a shorthand typist. She took her first job in Seaton. For many years she has lived in Sidmouth.

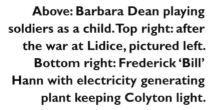

Above: Barbara Dean playing soldiers as a child. Top right: after the war at Lidice, pictured left. Bottom right: Frederick 'Bill' Hann with electricity generating plant keeping Colyton light.

Norman Williams

When everyone had gone, there were just me and another lad

We were just milling around waiting to be selected for a new home in Colyton, far from our proper homes in London. One by one, they all went. All the larger boys and girls seemed to go very quickly. I think the farmers were short of workers, so the senior boys of 13 and 14 went first. Then all the girls found homes. At 10, I was one of the youngest in the school and I was one of the last to be chosen.

When everyone had gone, there were just me and another lad, two years older, who went by the name of Albert Rooks. We were put in a car and driven to 22, Coly Vale, where we were billeted with Mr and Mrs Freddie White, waiting at home to see who was being thrust upon them.

Mrs White was a homely and kindly lady who made us very welcome and gave us a room where we shared the same bed. Her husband was a carpenter, whose father owned a butcher's shop next to the Gerrard Arms in St Andrew's Square. On Sundays, Mrs White attended the chapel in King Street and so I went too. For four years, that meant morning service, Sunday school in the afternoon and evening service.

I would sometimes be asked to pump the organ. I had to sit on a small bench at the back of it, lift a lever up and down and watch a piece of string carrying a lead weight. If the weight disappeared from view, you knew that the organ was being starved of air and would cease making a sound. Then you had to pump like blazes to get the sound back.

At the end of the service you would be given tuppence for your trouble. Between hymns you also had the opportunity to carve your initials on the back of the seat.

Mine are still there.

Norman Williams was an evacuee with St Jude's Church of England School, who moved with his mother from Reading just before the war. He moved back to the south-east towards the end of the war and later worked in transport and printing. In retirement, he now lives in the town of his birth.

Joan Dommett

We left for our honeymoon. It had been a very happy day, and now we were embarked on an adventure. For neither of us had ever stayed in a hotel

My story might never have had a happy ending had I not one day called into the coal depot at Colyton Station to pay a bill. For, there was Eddie paying his bill too.

We had known each other for some time. I would stop for a chat if I saw him trimming hedges or doing other jobs in the fields as I cycled down to Colyton from my home at Yardbury Hill.

By now I was 21 and working as a nanny with a family the other side of Taunton. Within a year or so, my country would be at war, yet life was pleasant, even if all the miles I did on my bicycle did sometimes make me weary.

After paying my bill I was to ride 29 miles back to the two little girls I looked after at Fitzroy Farm. It would take me two and a half hours. Eddie suggested he might ride some of the way with me and I agreed. It was the start of our romance.

Once a week for the next year Eddie and I would exchange letters and every fortnight he would cycle through Taunton to see me. Sometimes I would make the journey in the opposite direction to see Eddie and also my mother. Cycling was the only option.

Joan marries Eddie at a wartime ceremony in Colyton

A picture for the album: all the family line up for the camera

There was a bus but it cost 4s 6d, a big proportion of my 12s 6d weekly wage and it took just as long.

Usually when we met we would walk together. Occasionally there was an agricultural show or fair to go to. There wasn't much else to do.

Then, just after war had broken out, Eddie proposed. He didn't go down on one knee or anything like that. It might almost have been a business proposition. Eddie and his brother Frank had inherited Tritchmarsh Farm. His brother was also to marry but his girlfriend didn't want to live there because it was too close to relatives. Eddie said: 'This is our chance. Shall we take it? Shall we get married and work the farm?' The way he put it might not have been very romantic, but we were in love and it made sense. So I said yes.

We went by train to Axminster to buy a ring. The one we chose had three small diamonds. I was so proud of it.

It was to be 18 months before we married, and in the meantime the two boys continued to run the 77-acre farm between them. During that time we saved enough for the cows and machinery but not to buy Frank out of the farm. We tried to get a loan to cover Frank's half, but everyone turned us down. We were like a balloon pinched. It seemed our dream was over before it had begun. But Frank said we could pay him off quarterly after we married, and that's what we did. We worked our socks off until the farm was ours.

Our wedding was in 1941, on Easter Monday, because it was a sensible time in the farming calendar to start afresh. The ceremony was at midday at St Andrew's Church, where I had also been christened and confirmed. The bells rang out and people stopped to watch us leave the church.

By now the war was really beginning to bite, but the dresses weren't a problem. My own was made by Madame Wood, a dressmaker in Church Street, for whom I had worked at 5s a week when I left Colyton school at the age of 14. I was with her for four years until my first nanny's job at Seaton. Madame Wood knew what material she could get and what would suit me, and so I left the choice of dress to her. I knew her taste was good. She chose cream Georgette. I don't think I saw either the design or the material until my first fitting, and I had to cycle from Taunton for that. She also made my going-away outfit: a blue, striped dress with a plain blue coat. I felt nicer than I had ever felt. Everything was so lovely.

I had five bridesmaids. The dresses for the four children I made myself, including those for the two girls I looked after at Taunton. I cycled home with the dresses for my young sister and a cousin so they could be fitted properly. All the hems had to be generous so they could be let down to make party dresses as the girls grew older. My grown-up sister had hers made in London where she lived.

I cycled back from Taunton a week before the wedding to finalise everything.

Mum and I and my sisters prepared the food for the reception, which we held at my uncle's Little Downhayne Farm where my mother was now living. There were about 40 guests: family and special friends. We had sandwiches and sausage rolls; bread and cheese; jellies and trifles; and fruit salad. Quite a spread it was. It took us several hours to put it together.

The cake had to be iced chocolate, not white. There wasn't enough icing sugar available for baker Copp to give us two tiers of cake with royal icing. But there was enough to make white piping over the chocolate icing. It was delicious anyway, and it looked good. The top tier, with the chocolate icing scraped off, was saved, according to the tradition, for the first christening. But that was to be four and a half years in coming.

For the toast, there was a glass of wine, or port or sherry. There just wasn't the sort of drinking there is now.

By mid-afternoon, Eddie and I had left in his little car for our honeymoon. It had been a very happy day, and now we were embarked on an adventure. For, nothing had been booked, and neither of us had ever stayed in a hotel. In fact, Eddie's travels in Devon had never taken him farther than Honiton. He had never had a night off the farm. We decided on Torquay, and there we had three nights in the Belgrave Hotel. We did enjoy being waited upon. It was a real treat that was never to happen again. From then on, the farm came first, second and last.

The day we were back from our honeymoon we had 20 cows to milk, calves to feed and poultry and pigs to muck out. This was to be our life as a young married couple, seven days a week, 6am until it was dark.

Within weeks, we also found ourselves with a 'family' to care for.

Two evacuees arrived, one a 13-year-old girl from London called Pat Westwater and the other, a 12-year-old boy, Roy Graham, from Bristol. Pat was like a sister to me. Neither of them was the slightest trouble.

Though we had only recently been married, and money was short, we didn't mind having them with us at all. It was a pleasure seeing them enjoying the fresh air and having a life away from the bombs and the shortages, just as it was when holidaymakers began to arrive. We took trippers in for three guineas a week full board so that we could make ends meet. We had up to six of them at a time escaping the cities. It was such a relief for them that they hardly minded walking across the fields from Seaton Junction with their suitcases.

While they were with us, they didn't seem to do much but breathe in deeply and wonder at the quiet. They would often go no farther than the orchard, taking a rug to rest on. It was so different from the lives they led at home.

They didn't even mind the primitive conditions we lived in. If they were to wake in the night, they would have to make their way up the path to the nearest loo or use the jerry under the bed. We had no indoor sanitation. There was just one tap in the kitchen, from which jugs had to be filled to take upstairs – and for warm water there was just a top-up from the range.

We had no electricity either. At Fitzroy Farm, I had been used to having lights at the flick of a switch, flushing loos and running water. But at Tritchmarsh it was back to candles and later oil lamps. Electricity didn't come until 1960, and we weren't the last in the area even then.

We were the last, though, to have a tractor. Throughout the war, and indeed until 1962, we ploughed and rolled the fields, and did all our other jobs, with three working horses.

The one luxury we had was delivery of our food to the farm by pony and trap and later by van. Folletts, the grocer, would call for an order on Saturday and deliver on Monday. The bakers, Copps and Govers, would deliver three times a week. The butchers, Louds and Whites, would come on Tuesday with our weekday meat and collect our order for Sunday joints to be delivered on Saturday. Fresh fish would arrive with Reg Driver on his bike on Thursday morning.

As regular as clockwork, the postman would arrive daily across the fields from Seaton Junction. Our address then was Tritchmarsh, Shute. It was such a long walk just to reach us, and sometimes in winter the floods would thwart him. So they decided to send a postman out from Colyton by bike, and our address became Tritchmarsh, Colyton. If we posted a letter at Three Sycamores to my sister in London on Sunday afternoon, it always arrived with her by Monday afternoon.

Despite these conveniences, the war years, and those afterwards, were tough by modern standards. They were often cold and uncomfortable. They were certainly dark and sometimes grim. But we were young and energetic and we took no notice of it all. Life was what we made it, though we did welcome the long summer nights.

For our visitors from the cities, Tritchmarsh was a shelter in the storm. It was our privilege to live there all the time, no matter what the hardships.

Joan Dommett had three daughters, one of whom, Christine, lives with her at Tritchmarsh. Together they have kept the land farmed since Eddie's death in 1996.

Maureen Turner

My mother's wicker basket toppled over and its precious Bramley apples began rolling down the hill. Up she leapt to catch them as the plane turned and headed towards us

Suddenly, skimming the rooftops to our left, a German bomber roared across us from the sea. I gasped as I saw the iron cross painted on its side. Then, to my horror, the bomb doors opened.

'Look mum,' I shouted, as a bomb dropped towards houses below, 'there's a German plane.' She picked me up and chucked me in the gutter, then lay over me in what would probably have been a futile attempt to give me some protection.

I knew all about German planes and what they could do to people they attacked. Only a few months earlier I had been growing up in London. I had seen the skies blood-red from the fires their bombs had started, and night after night I had been with 20 or so other people sheltering in the cellar of my father's pub, near Brixton.

I was seven and already a nervous wreck.

My older brother was on the fire floats on the Thames. He said it was getting too dangerous for us to stay in London. Take the two girls, he demanded of our mother, and get out into the country. So in 1941 we had come to Seaton to escape the war.

And here I was on 12 August 1942, a lovely sunny day, lying

petrified in Seaton Down Road as a house blew up one street to our left and people were being machine-gunned on the pavement one street to our right.

My mother's wicker basket toppled over and its load of precious Bramley apples began rolling down the hill. Up she leapt to catch them as the plane turned and headed down the street, now apparently shooting at us. A woman opened her cottage door and we dived for the cover we had been offered.

The plane swung back out to sea and was gone. It had been another of the hit-and-run raids on Seaton. John and May Eeles, two evacuees living with them, Stella and June Moore, and a visitor, 91-year-old Elizabeth Woolacott, had died in the shattered house in Highwell Road. Mrs Walton, my piano teacher's sister and the widow of the church organist, had perished in the machine-gunning in Townsend Road.

Mr Eeles had been a member of the Home Guard, which three days later paraded at his funeral led by a vicar who was an ARP warden. Among the mourners were the children's parents from Plumstead in London. Shortly before their deaths, the children had pleaded with them to return home. Stella had been identified from a ring bearing a picture of a pixie and shown to a playmate spared from the blast because he had been late for tea.

When we arrived back at our house in Townsend we found that the front door had been blown in and had struck my sister. She was sitting bruised and badly shaken. Above her, the ceiling had been peppered with bullets. The holes ran across the plaster like stitching in a frock.

Having fled London's bombing, we had been caught up in a terrifying experience in supposedly peaceful Devon. We had jumped from the frying pan into the fire and we were lucky to have survived.

Our attackers scuttled off home but some paid the price. One German plane that had been shot down was paraded in Seaton like a trophy. Minus its wings, it sat on the back of an articulated lorry parked in Harbour Road, where the fish and chip is now. It was presumably there for its propaganda value, showing local people that the Germans weren't having it all their own way. Looking inside, I saw a bloodied sock. It has stayed in my mind all these years; navy blue, it was, with a ribbed top. We were never to know what happened to the crew but the blood carried its own message: the pain and suffering of war visited both sides.

Had my mother got her own way, there would have been rather more. For beside the back door leaned a garden fork, and her gruesome instruction was to stick it straight into the stomach of any German parachutist I was to see.

Something of what I had been told nearly led to my own downfall. One day a friend and I were playing at being parachutists. We climbed on to the verandah with umbrellas and leapt off, believing our fall would be broken. Instead we hit the ground with a thud. Our bumps and scratches reinforced mother's warning never to do it again.

By now I had become a child of my wartime environment. When I was being a nuisance at home, I would be put on guard duty out in the street. I dressed in khaki-coloured trousers, boots and a tin hat and carried a wooden gun, and I thought I was a hell of a dog. I'd march up and down outside the house for hours, quite convinced I was doing a really worthwhile job.

Seaton had become a playground for us kids. Down on the beach there was all we needed to keep us entertained. Concrete blocks had been put at intervals on top of what was then a low sea wall. Out of each one stuck a metal spike, and connecting all these was barbed wire. But a gap had been left for the fishermen to get down to the water with their boats, and of course that let us on to the beach too. There, a barrier had been built to stop tanks being landed, and we used to climb to the top of it. It was especially good fun in rough weather when the waves would crash over us. Had my mother known she would have died a thousand deaths.

It wasn't the only dangerous game we had. A landing craft had beached on the pebbles and broken in half. A hole had been cut in the deck so that the engine could be rescued, and that had filled with water. We loved playing on the wreck, especially jumping over the hole in the deck. What would have happened if one of us had ever fallen in doesn't bear thinking about.

At the top of the beach, the fisherman had a capstan, into which a dozen tree trunks had been slotted. From this a hawser ran down the beach and would be hooked to a returning boat so that it could be hauled clear of the tide line. We would help to push the capstan round and round to drag the boat up the beach. We thought ourselves so grown up.

While all this was going on we would leave our mothers' shopping baskets, with our ration books and all the precious food we had bought, and no-one would ever touch them.

We had the freedom of the town, quite unlike children today. The best fun of all was travelling with the coalman. He was a lovely man with pebble glasses perched on his blackened face. Over his shoulder he wore a leather pad to protect himself from the heavy sacks he had to hump off the back of the lorry and into people's sheds. I would jump up into his cab and be taken everywhere around town.

For long periods, the holiday camp was full of soldiers, in turn British, Czechs, Poles and Americans. I loved the Czechs and adored the Americans who succeeded them. They were all so nice to children. The Czechs had presents to give us from their government exiled in Britain. One was a book of fairy tales, which I still have somewhere. We were given stamps to collect too, and one soldier made me a bow and arrow I treasured.

The local Catholic priest would appeal to parishioners to take home soldiers and give them lunch, so most Sundays my mother would come back from church with two or three. We got to know some of them really well. For a while after he left, my mother wrote regularly to one of them but soon after the war he pleaded with her not to do so again because he said it was dangerous for him to know us now the Communists were in charge of his country. So regrettably that was a friend lost.

Our best friends were the Americans. Their accent beguiled us and their uniform was so smooth, unlike the rough fabric our own troops had to wear. To us, they were just exotic.

Generosity was their trademark. They gave us sweets and chewing gum, which was a novelty to me. They handed out badges and insignia. They played with us and took us for rides in their jeeps. My sister, who was eight years older than me, was swept off her feet by them. Several of them became her boyfriends.

Like the Czechs before them they would come for Sunday lunch and some at other times too. Our favourite was Frank Schultz, who was half native-American. He had a squat nose and swarthy skin and came from the south, so he had an attractive drawl. We saw a lot of him. He was so good to me.

When the Americans pulled out to prepare for the D-Day invasion, Frank came to say goodbye. It was all hugs and tears. Then they were gone. The town was full of them one day and empty the next.

We never heard from Frank again. Sadly, he was probably killed on one of the French beaches.

In many ways, the war was so much fun. But I missed my dad, who had stayed in London to run the pub, and it was hard to say farewell to soldier friends we doubted we'd ever see again.

So farmer George Retter became our new friend. He was a big fat man with a little wife and they would come in a pony and trap from Colyton to sell their produce. My mother bought food from him on the doorstep and he said he would come every week, which he did.

She felt sorry for them and would invite them in for a cup of tea, much to the annoyance of the snooty retired colonel who lived next door and disapproved of nearly everything, including hawkers from the countryside. He said no good would come of mother's hospitality, but it did.

For, after we had gone back to London in 1946, food was scarce and Farmer Retter knew it. So every Christmas for some years he sent us a big brown parcel containing a leg of pork and as much food as he could cram around it, which we were sure he wasn't supposed to do.

A little kindness had gone a long, long way.

Maureen with an eye to the future

One of Maureen Turner's early jobs back in London after the war was on the buses. For three years she was a conductress crossing the capital from Crystal Palace to Golders Green. She learned to fly Tiger Moth biplanes and was known as the Flying Clippie. Later, when her family moved to Cornwall she trained as a nurse and became director of nursing services at Treliske Hospital, Truro. Twenty years ago she retired to Colyton where she continues to live.

Jim Board

Hubert's letter, like so many before it, had distressingly been holed by the censor. It was as if some of him, some of what belonged to her, had been scratched away

Her longed-for letter fluttered to the floor at home in Colyton. It was an airmail letter from somewhere in North Africa, but instinctively mother knew that. It meant my eldest brother Hubert was still alive and safe.

For her, gripping these scraps of paper tightly in her hand was like holding him close to her again. She would read them over and over again as relief came in deep sighs.

Hubert, her eldest son, had been away at war since reaching his 18th birthday in 1939. She had seen him just once and then only briefly on embarkation leave as he departed for the Eighth Army in the desert. She wouldn't see him again until it was all over. The passage of more than five years would be very slow indeed.

His photograph stood on the sideboard. When he had left, she didn't have one. Ordinary families like ours didn't have cameras. There had been only her memory of him to sustain her, how he had looked the day of his departure for goodness knows where. But with the last letter had come this picture of her boy growing into a man, surrounded by his mates, his hand against a tank, his face clearly tanned by the sun.

Brother Hubert, away for more than five years, with Alan, top right, Sidney, centre right, and Denis, bottom right

I also missed my brother but not with a mother's intensity. I missed the other three, too, Alan in Italy, Sidney in France and Denis somewhere at sea. By 1943 I had four brothers at war; my mother had four sons, and there lay a crucial difference. It gnawed at her every day.

In turn, as each one left in uniform, there had been a restrained farewell. There was duty to be done, and mother and son both knew it. The house remained full of children and others came along to fill the sorrow gap. Altogether, mother had 14 of us, though sadly four of my brothers and sisters were not to survive long into childhood. She loved us all, but for those who were away in danger her love was laced with a constant anxiety: could they possibly live through whatever they were having to endure?

Hubert's letter, like so many before it, was holed distressingly by the censor. It was as if some of him, some of what belonged to her, had been scratched away. No doubt the army had its reasons for being so careful, and these were greater than any compassion its officers had for people like my mother.

Hers was the grinding, every-minute-of-every-day reality of war being fought not only on battlefields overseas, but also on the intimate level of mothers worrying about the children wrenched from them. Her distress became less bearable as families in Colyton began to hear of their menfolk being killed in action. A pall of sadness descended on the town and seeped into our own home.

Our father, too, will have felt the pain of sons so far from home, but his suffering wasn't as visible. In those days, men didn't display their affection as they do today. Their role in the family was more distinct. Father earned the daily bread for his large family and had to work very hard as a tree feller to do it. That was as far as it usually went, though there were times when the value of his support for my mother was immense.

He had to stay at home while his sons went off to fight, but he was required to join the Home Guard, which he hated. As children we had great fun at the expense of this motley crew, falling in behind them and mocking their marching skills, much to the annoyance of the officer in charge. One evening I saw some of them fall in on parade straight out of the White Hart pub. They were on their way to Axmouth Cliff for guard duty and had a bottle or two in their pockets for the night ahead.

Father was a proud man. He would have felt humiliated in public being laughed at by the local kids and perhaps by some of their elders too. But, if you missed many of the parades, however good your excuses, you might have to explain your absence to the magistrates and face a fine for abrogating what they regarded as your civic duty. He would stick to the task.

When I left school in 1942, I was directed by the Seaton labour exchange into war effort of my own. Along with brother Denis, who had not yet been called up, I had to report nine miles away at Dunkeswell airfield, where we were put on the maintenance team, mending broken windows among other jobs.

Here we were to meet the US Navy and watch their preparations for D-Day. We saw Americans at work and at play. They loved their old motor bikes, souped up with aviation fuel, and practising their rifle shooting on rabbits. But it wasn't all fun. Planes would return from engaging the enemy with all sorts of damage. One couldn't get its under-carriage down and crash-landed. The crew survived, but four men on fire duty perished when their jeep crashed as it sped to the rescue.

The foreman, a Colyton man called Bill Hussey, had a special job for us one day. He told us to paint this vast hangar. He instructed us to wire-brush it down, tar it and then paint it, using the two quart-sized billy-cans and three-inch paint brushes he gave us. For this stupendous job, we would be paid 3d a square yard.

We began to do as we had been told and then realised the war would be long over by the time we finished, so we put our heads together. At the American stores, they gave us two sweeping brushes, one for each of us, and two buckets. We dipped our brooms into the buckets filled with tar from 50-gallon barrels and covered three square yards almost in one movement. As a result, my next wage packet contained £32, a huge sum in those days; nearly 10 years later, now as a married man, my wage was only

£5 a week. I thought I was in paradise, but it wasn't to last long. The clerk of works twigged what we were doing and instantly put an end to our money-making.

Americans were our new neighbours in Colyton, too. They were nothing if not generous with what they had and we didn't. In the pubs they spent their money on the girls who had once been content with lesser treats from the local boys. So they were popular with their new girlfriends but often met hostility from the young men.

Some wives fraternised with them. Babies were born when husbands were far away. Hearts were broken. And gossip was rife. It was wartime and anything might have happened, and some of it did. Perhaps least said, the better.

In 1939, when there were nine of us living at home, we moved from a two-bedroom house in Lower Church Street, then Cross Street, to the Compasses, a big thatched building at the top of the town in South Street. Until recently it had been a pub. One night my father and I were standing on the doorstep when a German plane skimmed the rooftops and fired down the street, its bullets scuffing the tarmac. We hustled inside quickly.

Another came very low over the school playing fields and Betty, the sister of the girl who was to become my wife, took a shrapnel wound. That might have been the plane that ditched at Little Downhayne. We were soon at the site of that crash on our bikes, scavenging for souvenirs. But what we collected was straightaway confiscated by our parents and thrown away. They didn't want anything from the war that had stolen their sons away.

None of these incidents bore the slightest comparison with the terrible bombing of Exeter, which I witnessed from a hospital window.

I had not been on a train before, or even out of Colyton, when

I had to report to the eye infirmary, now a hotel in Magdalen Road, having been wounded by a dart carelessly thrown at the youth club. The second night I was there, explosions across the city terrified me. Looking out of the window, all you could see was burning. For a boy from a quiet backwater it was an awful experience, as it was of course for everyone else. Here the war was real. Yet somehow it seemed as if it was not, that what was happening out there was happening in some sort of impossible fantasy world. We watched as bodies were brought to a makeshift mortuary in the grounds. One lad hardly able to comprehend what he was seeing left the ward to walk beside the trolleys, touching them as if to make sure that it all was real.

Back home after the Exeter blitz, the war continued to pass us by. The invasion threat at Seaton evaporated. Air raids were even fewer. My evacuee friend, Jim France, had gone back to London because his father believed he was being used as cheap labour by a farmer. Late in the war, his house there was hit by a flying bomb and he lost a leg, a devastating injury from which he never recovered and which he always blamed on his father.

We were more fortunate. Our food was rationed but we never went short of things to eat, in part because rationing favoured big families. Meat had been a rarity for us before the war; we just couldn't afford it. Nor were we used to having sweets. Now father worked overtime to put vegetables on our table year round from a large garden and two allotments - and there were rabbits to trap in the fields, pigeons to shoot from the sky and fish to catch in the river.

Just as before, mother's waiting war continued to take its toll. You could sense her fretting about where her sons were, how they were, whether they were safe. Every month, without fail, she would write to them and will her letters to reach them. Their replies dropped through the letterbox at home creating a bridge between them. They were all still alive.

And alive they fortunately stayed. They returned as I was called up. But by then the war had ended. There were no banners or balloons, no ostentatious homecoming. It was enough to have them back.

In town, the relief was palpable as people gave their good news to anyone and everyone. It was a time of great rejoicing.

Throughout the war, Colyton's people had cared for one another and shared what they had, including their sorrows and their anxieties. Now their boys had come home, at least those who were not later to have their names carved into the memorial in St Andrew's churchyard.

My mother's prayers had been answered. Her waiting war was over.

Jim Board was called up in 1946 to become the fifth brother to serve overseas. After demob in 1948, he worked on a farm and then became a postman, retiring to live as he had always done, in Colyton. His book on his childhood, The River Runs By, has sold 3,000 copies.

Stella Marks

A life of ordinariness lay behind her, but one that had included three years of an extraordinary experience shared by an army of girls who fought their war on the land

My mother's young life had been tainted by death at every turn. So many of her family had died while she was growing up that it was bound to have a bearing on the decisions she made as an adult.

But by the time the young Olive Hawkins, of Eyewell Green, Seaton, had made up her mind what she would do to contribute herself to the war effort yet more hurdles were put in her way.

First it had been her mother who had died from TB. Olive had been only six then. So her older sister Hilda, who was 17, set about bringing her up. Hilda was a strong-minded young woman used to getting her own way. She was the big sister, well aware of her responsibilities to the child without a mother and determined to carry them out fully.

At 15 Olive lost her father, a soldier knocked off his bike and killed just before the war. Two sisters had already died and a brother would be her family's second TB victim within four months.

Father had served in the First World War and had been about to serve in the second. Her surviving brother would soon be called up.

Olive Hawkins, left, and, right, with dominant sister Hilda

As Olive grew into womanhood she had her own sense of duty. Like many other women she wanted to make a difference. By 1943, as she approached her 20th birthday, there were 80,000 in the Women's Land Army, 1,700 of them in Devon. My mother decided that she would join them.

All those deaths had given significance to the security of the home her sister had made for her. But Hilda dominated her too much, much as fathers and mothers everywhere dominated their daughters in those days. Young women were tied to the home and expected to follow domestic routines and the usual routes into marriage and motherhood.

The war was changing all that by throwing down expectations of its own. As food became increasingly difficult to import, more of it needed to be produced on farms at home. Yet most able-bodied men were away fighting and so farmers had few available people to help make their land more productive.

Enlisting an army of women was seen as the answer. The Land Army, often referred to as the Forgotten Army, had actually been formed in 1917 when food was scarce in the First World War. It had been re-formed in 1939 when girls were encouraged to join with advertising slogans and even a song:

Back to the land, we must all lend a hand.
To the farms and the fields we must go.
There's a job to be done,
Though we can't fire a gun.
We can still do our bit with the hoe . . .
Back to the land, with its clay and its sand,
Its granite and gravel and grit,
You grow barley and wheat
And potatoes to eat
To make sure that the nation keeps fit . . .
We will tell you once more
You can help win the war
If you come with us back to the land.

Girls often travelled long distances to the farms to which they had been allocated. From Colyton, some found themselves as far away as Herefordshire, living with the farmer's family or collectively in hostels. Others came here from homes in other parts of the country.

Olive chose to stay in her own home but desperately wanted her place in the war. First she had to convince the authorities that her back condition, a curvature of the spine, would allow her to undertake the heavy work. She was turned down, but fought on until eventually she was accepted. She must have had such character. You can see it in her face from the photographs that survived the war.

Pictures from the scrap book. Above, Land Army girls in full uniform and, below, taking a break from work on the farm

She was given a uniform of two short-sleeved shirts, a tie, a green pullover, two pairs of socks, a pair of shoes, a bib and brace overall, a hat, a pair of rubber boots and a long mackintosh for the winter and sent to Mounthill Farm, on the Whitford road out of Colyton.

She travelled daily by bus to start unfamiliar work at 8am, milking cows by hand, ploughing the land with horses, tending the pigs and poultry, planting and digging up potatoes, haymaking and harvesting corn. On the farm was another Land Army girl. The farmer, Mark Sweetland, would start one girl at one end of the field thinning out root crops with a hoe and the other at the opposite end so they wouldn't waste time talking.

For the work that was often gruelling and sometimes monotonous, Olive, like the others, was paid 10d an hour, two pence less than a man. But she was happy and she was valued. She made good relationships with the farmer's family and with other girls who worked locally. There was a great sense of camaraderie among them all. The tasks asked of them were difficult and unrelenting, sometimes physically challenging, but they were all pulling together in common cause.

In January1946, after the war had been won, Olive was released from the Land Army to marry Marwood Soper, a petty officer in the Royal Navy from Axmouth. Outside St Gregory's Church, Seaton, girls from the local Land Army club formed a guard of honour with pitchforks. Nine of them had signed a card wishing her well and the club presented her with a dinner service.

The following month, at a club dinner, 20 of the girls and three Land Army officials signed a souvenir card.

These cards now form part of my collection of mementoes from my mother's life. She achieved so much against all the odds, those many deaths she endured at such tender ages and her own

By this personal message I wish to express to you

Miss Olive Hawkins,

my appreciation of your loyal and devoted service
as a member of the Women's Land Army from
July,1943, *to* January,1946.
Your unsparing efforts at a time when the victory
of our cause depended on the utmost use of the
resources of our land have earned for you the
country's gratitude.

Elizabeth R

medical condition.

Later, with my father at sea so much of the time, she brought up two children mostly on her own and, like every other mother, cooked, sewed, knitted and gardened. Unlike most, though, she had memories of a life different from anything that had gone before or came afterwards. She treasured her time on the farm and was proud to have served her country.

She never forgot the people she worked with. And she was never forgotten. At her ruby wedding anniversary, a card came from Mounthill Farm with the congratulations of those she had worked for. She returned her thanks with a telephone call.

Five years later she was dead, a life of ordinariness behind her, one that had been touched by so much sadness but had included three years of an extraordinary experience shared by an army of girls who fought their war on the land.

In my collection I have the personal message that must have been one of the earliest to be signed by the Queen.

As all the other Land Army girls will know, those who worked in this part of Devon and those who toiled many miles away, that message told my mother:

'Your unsparing efforts at a time when the victory of our cause depended on the utmost use of the resources of our land have earned for you the country's gratitude.'

After the war, Olive Hawkins moved from Seaton to Axmouth. When her husband was invalided out of the navy, they took over the Red Lion pub at Membury. Stella was the first of two children, born in 1947. She lives at South Chard.

Aileen Sydenham

Farm labourers would start drinking at one end of the town and finish at the other

By the time of the war, the number of pubs in Colyton had declined from 11 to six. My parents, Charlie and Bessie Warren, kept one of those to be closed after peace had returned, the Country House Inn on Sidmouth Road, opposite what was then the Co-op and now is the CeramTec factory.

It was a brewery pub and my father ran it for 46 years before it was turned into a private house.

Father was a man of many parts. He was a baker as well as a publican, working through the night at the Co-op. He was also a taxi driver, and he reared pigs, poultry and cows on a smallholding on some of the land where the factory now stands. Mother made cheese from the milk and blackpot (black pudding), chitlings (pigs' intestines), pasties and other meat products. They never stopped.

For many years the pub sold nothing but beer and cider, but eventually father obtained a spirits licence and broadened the range of drinks he could sell. Beer came at 6d a pint and cider at 3d.

The public bar ran across the front of the pub, with a fire in the middle of the room around which people sat, and barrels lined up behind the bar supported by gibs. In the back was a taproom, where games were played, table skittles and darts. Upstairs, five bedrooms and a bathroom would accommodate paying guests at 2s 6d a night. The huge breakfasts, offering whatever the customer wanted, were alone worth the money. Yet I remember one cyclist refusing to pay so much and mother having to threaten him with the police.

The pub's customers were mainly people living near the pub, but especially at weekends farm labourers would start at one end of the town and finish at the other, visiting them all.

Tripe suppers were served every month or so. They were delicious. The tripe would be prepared with onions and a thick sauce and served with chunks of bread. Sometimes another pub's customers would be invited for games and a tripe supper. They were great occasions.

After Dunkirk, soldiers were billeted at the pub. Twelve or 15 were put up in the stables and two officers with their batmen had rooms upstairs. The army didn't know what to do with so many men returning at once from France. The soldiers made themselves useful but the officers kept themselves to themselves and were looked after by their batmen.

Sometimes when the officers were out, mother would sit the soldiers around the fire in the pub and serve them cakes she had made.

Such wonderful days they were.

By the end of the war, Aileen Sydenham was married and subsequently had two children. Later, when she lost her husband, she worked for many years at the CeramTec factory. She has always lived in Colyton.

Nigel Speller

We took turns for fire-watching. One moonlit night I saw a German plane come in low. There was a rattle of machine-gun fire as the pilot aimed at cattle in the field

There we were, line abreast, schoolboys searching for bombs in a cornfield back from the cliffs. It was a good job our parents didn't know.

The Germans had dropped butterfly bombs. Beware of them, posters warned us all. They were designed to blow up when someone touched one of their 'wings'.

I was 16 or 17 and a senior pupil at Allhallows, a boarding school above the sea at Rousdon, between Axminster and Lyme Regis.

Our headmaster, who had been in the Indian Army, was a community-minded sort of chap who wanted his school to help the war effort. He thought it would benefit the boys, too.

He had been asked by the local constabulary if we might go looking for the bombs. Policemen would walk behind us and stick a pole in the ground next to any we found. Then the bomb disposal people would come along and detonate them safely.

Of course, it wouldn't be allowed now. But, in the war, attitudes were different. The field had to be cleared so the corn could be harvested. The corn would have been too valuable to waste. As long as we were careful we were told we wouldn't be in any danger.

So about a dozen of us were pulled out of lessons and, excitedly, lined up in the summer sunshine to walk gingerly across the field in the Combpyne valley, our eyes peeled for suspicious-looking objects. And we found them. Several bombs were marked and later dealt with. There were no casualties.

All through the war we schoolboys had done our bit. My first job, I remember, had been as a 12 or 13-year-old pulling out ragwort from the field of the Pinhay Estate, then owned by the chairman of governors, Major Ormsby Allhusen, for ever afterwards known as Major Ragwort. Ragwort would have poisoned his cattle.

I had been too young in 1940 to join the detail ordered to dig a tank ditch on the lane down to Charton Point. But a dozen of the older boys spent more than 24 hours trying to hinder the expected invasion.

The lane had been constructed by the Peek family before their mansion became our new school after its move from Honiton. They had wanted to recover Italian marble from a shipwreck and needed a way of hauling it up from the shore. The marble made a lovely staircase. There must have been so much of it that they used it for almost anything. Even shelves and tables in the dairy were marble.

This stretch of coast was thought a likely invasion point. Later it emerged that we had indeed been in direct line of attack under a German invasion plan called Operation Sea Lion. So, if they had landed, German tanks would have had to be stopped heading up the lane. In truth, the ditch might have halted a light carrier and nothing more.

Almost from the start there had been the sights and sounds of war, though some of them may seem a little ridiculous to many people now. The first local defence volunteers, mainly elderly men and some of the senior boys, formed up in the quadrangle armed with nothing more than pikes and staves. They had rallied to Anthony Eden's call in 1940 to guard the home shores.

They saw their first action within a week. They were called out of their classes when German parachutists were reported. The enemy turned out to be farmworkers, haversacks on their backs, returning home. The LDV practised with what weaponry they had, including Mills bombs (grenades) and stored Molotov cocktails in secret dumps along the cliff-top. A scare over the coast guard being kidnapped by a German patrol ended with the door of his hut being kicked in. There he sat startled almost to death.

By the time the LDV became the Home Guard, it had become a force to be reckoned with, because of fuller training and better weaponry. Its skills were tested by a mine floating towards the beach. Several senior boys were in the party sent to the cliff-top to assemble and fire a Hotchkiss machine gun. The mine was clearly visible bobbing on the waves offshore. Careful aim was taken, the order given and the trigger squeezed. The barrel shot forward six inches and fell off. The 'mine' turned out to be an empty oil drum.

Firewatching was a regular duty for older boys. Every night through the war we would take turns in pairs to climb the tower for two-hour stints. Then we would return to our beds. One moonlit night I was on top of the tower and saw a German plane come in low to the east towards Pinhay. There was a rattle of machine-gun fire as the pilot aimed at cattle in the field, but he didn't hit any.

Towards the end of the war I was trusted to be an air raid warden. It was nothing like as glamorous as being in the Home Guard but I was trained to fight fires with a stirrup pump and I was given an armband. It made me feel I had my own role in the school's war effort.

In 1944 I passed 17 and could drive a car. There were none of today's driving lessons. I was just put in a car and, without the qualified passenger you have to have now, I was left to pick up driving skills as I went along. My housemaster had a Morris Oxford, and he was in charge of the local Home Guard. So he made me useful by having me run errands in the car between the school and Home Guard headquarters in Seaton.

I soon learned to drive, though I didn't take a test until much later when I was in the army. And I learned to conserve the master's precious petrol ration by free-wheeling down the hill from Rousdon. You just switched off the engine and would get all the way to the Axe, just beyond Axmouth church, before having to switch it on again.

Other than these trips, getting around was always uncomfortable. From my parents' home near London I took the train for school terms. I'd change at Axminster and catch the Lyme Regis 'flyer', getting off at Combpyne. From there I would walk with my suitcase to school. The heavy stuff would be sent 'luggage in advance' at a cost of 2s and generally arrive two days later in a pretty dilapidated lorry.

I had my bicycle at school and would use it to explore the countryside, which was easier said than done. Because of the fear of invasion, all the signposts had been removed. They didn't want invading Germans to find their way around conveniently. Once, having ridden into Colyton, I couldn't find my way out again. It was a long time before I found the right road back to school.

We might have been largely out of harm's way at Allhallows but we followed the war assiduously. That was probably because we realised that one day we might be involved ourselves, depending how long the fighting was to last. I took *The War Illustrated* every week and still have bound copies. And perhaps because we were at school we would trace progress on maps. I was an avid listener to Winston Churchill's periodic Sunday night speeches on the wireless. I particularly remember him telling us that Germany had invaded Russia and that the Russians were now our allies. That helped to make me realise how much the world had become engulfed by war.

Often at our daily chapel services we would hear about casualties, old boys who had been killed or who were missing. Sometimes their families would make gifts to the chapel in memory of their loved ones

We would see the planes overhead and the ships moving up and down the Channel so we were always conscious of things happening to other people, even when we were in the school chapel in the crypt beneath the Great Hall. I was confirmed there at the age of 14 by the Bishop of Exeter. During the service, fighters were engaged in a dogfight overhead but the service wasn't interrupted. We couldn't detect the noise of their firing but we could hear the spent cartridges clattering on the roof above. Later we were allowed to go up and collect the cartridge cases. I picked up one and kept it for a long time.

As the D-Day invasion approached, the school found itself in a restricted area reaching back 10 miles from the coast. The authorities wanted to prevent people seeing the preparations being made but we had a view of all the shipping. For the whole of one day in June 1944 we could see through binoculars the horizon full of naval ships of the invasion armada moving up the Channel towards the Normandy landing zone. From this and from all the troops in the area, British and American, it had been clear something big was about to happen. It was exciting to think how all the early defeats of the war might now be reversed once and for all. And we were among the first to catch a glimpse of what was about to happen.

I had decided I wanted to go into the army. Men were being called up for work in the mines and I wanted to avoid that. So I took myself off to Exeter, to the recruiting office that was part of the empty Plaza Cinema, and enlisted as a volunteer. They put me on a reserve list and sent me back to school.

Growing up away from home in wartime had been an interesting experience. Hardships had been few. We had been fed reasonably well, had cakes and buns in the tuck shop from Gills' bakery in Axminster, milk from the home farm and sometimes even cream teas at 1s 3d a time from the Gapper family's cottage in the Undercliff.

But I have special reason to remember one meal. To stretch our meat rations, the school decided to feed us rabbit, all 200 of us. Imagine how many rabbits that would have required, and how old some of them must have been when they were served to us. Some of them must have been the walking dead.

I have never liked the wretched things since.

After the war Nigel Speller was commissioned as an officer in the army. He rose to the rank of brigadier and became the army's director of movements. He retired in 1979 to work for the Church of England in the Exeter diocese, having already taken a house in Colyton when his son and daughter followed him to Allhallows. He is now a lay reader in the Colyton benefice.

Gerald Goddard

She would rush through the streets blowing her whistle so people could take shelter. When the danger had passed she would boom 'All cle-ar, all cle-ar' in her posh voice

His name was Herbert Breiter, Private First Class 32652500. I shall always remember his name and number.

He was an American soldier billeted in Colyton while the generals prepared for the D-Day landings, and he was my friend.

On pay day Herbert and the others would shoot crap on the pavement outside Church House in the Market Place, where the officers were based, sometimes losing all they had been given on the turn of the dice. They generally had more money than they knew what to do with.

The American soldiers lived at The Grove in South Street for a year from 1943, and my friends and I, all of us about12 or 13, would go to one place or the other for a chat and for the chewing gum they would give us. Or, for anything we could get, if I'm honest.

I looked forward to seeing Herbert. He was friendly and generous, and he seemed to like me.

The day came, of course, when he and the others packed their kit and were gone. We waved them goodbye sitting on the wall outside Goodings the plumbers in what was then called East Street and got on with other things, as kids do.

For a start we broke into The Grove to see what the Americans had left behind. We were teenagers by now, though no-one ever used the term, and we were streetwise. I found a softball which I have to this day. Herbert and the others had taught us how to play baseball and so for a while the ball was used for our own games. In Church House the only discovery was a duck's egg.

From time to time Herbert would continue to send me parcels of candy from wherever his unit was stationed on the continent and I would acknowledge the gifts with letters of thanks, using the rank and number I've never forgotten.

Then, quite suddenly it seemed, there were no more parcels. I reckoned the poor devil had been killed.

With the departure of the Americans came the end of other treats. We lived at Tickens House, next to where the fire station is now. Then it was a sawmill. Opposite was Clapps Farm where now there's an old people's home. My mother was friendly with the farmer, Fred Wilmington, who would collect the food waste from the Americans' canteen at the White Cottage in Dolphin Street, supposedly to feed to his pigs. But before the pigs put a snout to the trough we would sift through what had been thrown out. The Americans had their food shipped in and they lived exceptionally well. They wasted what we never saw, bananas and oranges and the like. It wasn't that we were hungry. We were never short of food that could be grown or shot in the fields. But we hadn't anything that would have to come from far away. To get any of that was special.

Before the Americans, British soldiers had come in their hundreds from Dunkirk. Czechs and Poles followed them. Colyton had never seen so many people. Its streets had always been empty,

I remember; few of the cars you see everywhere now, perhaps an occasional horse and cart. The soldiers certainly filled the six pubs, and the girls loved having them around. As kids we did too. They were so much fun.

Early in the war, one British soldier even taught me how to swim. In those days, Colyton had its own pool. It was up a lane and across the fields from Chantry Bridge. There was a sluice gate to draw in water from the Umborne, where cattle would sometimes paddle, and to let it out again, when all the green slime was cleaned off the walls. The kids would congregate at the pool in summer. I was nine or 10 at the time and a soldier, whose name I never knew, taught me how to swim. I actually became quite a strong swimmer and have him to thank for that. After the war, the pool was closed for public health reasons, though I don't recall any of us ever being ill from playing in the water.

The war created its own friendships. For two or three years, we had evacuees with us from London, and I've had contact with them at intervals ever since. One was Rene Smith, a bright boy who went on to own a garage business. He passed 'the scholarship' here and thought he was going to Colyton Grammar School, but instead the authorities insisted he had to go all the way to Newton Abbot. He didn't want to leave my mother and refused the offer of a place.

The other was Reg Robinson, whose family background was really very difficult. He couldn't read or write, and my stepfather, Sam Quance, taught him. Reg went on to make a success of himself, too, and was always grateful for the help he had been given while he was staying with us. Many years later when Sam died, Reg came to his funeral.

Rene and Reg attended school in the town hall until remaining evacuees – many went home during the lull in bombing after the Battle of Britain - were mixed with the local children at the council school. In those early years of the war when Colyton feared bombing raids, we would be warned of planes heading our way by a local dignitary called Mrs Tyson. She was the billeting officer, and she ran the WI, too; a very formidable lady who liked to be in charge. Everyone knew her and seemed rather afraid of her. She would rush through the streets blowing her whistle so people could take shelter. When the danger had passed, she would be out again booming 'All cle-ar, all cle-ar' in her posh voice.

One evening at this time, our doctor was given a hero's welcome at the town hall. Dr Aveling had joined the army and been captured in Norway. Early in the war there was some sort of deal over exchanging prisoners who were doctors. So the British gave up a German doctor and got Dr Aveling in return. He came back to Colyton's cheers.

The school was moved out of the hall so that it could become a store for cattle cake. From then until the end of the war it was filled floor to ceiling with sheets of this linseed-oil cake ready for its distribution to local farmers. Afterwards, the floor was fantastic for dancing because of the oil that had seeped from the sheets.

Upstairs, the ARP (Air Raid Precautions), led by my stepfather, would spend nights watching from the windows for fires caused by incendiaries. These would be dropped by German planes returning from bombing missions over Bristol and Cardiff. They were not so much aiming at us as dumping their remaining bombs so they would be unencumbered by their weight as they crossed the Channel back home. One night, a field at Kingsdon, near the station, was set alight by a great many incendiaries. We all rushed to see this spectacular sight. But there were no casualties, and only one bomb did any damage. It fell quite harmlessly through the station roof.

We kids treated our wartime experience as an enjoyable adventure. Within minutes of something happening, a group of us would appear on our bikes ready for mischief. To us, it might have been something out of an Enid Blyton story.

We were all lads at the grammar school, which might have approved of some of our enterprise, but would certainly not have sanctioned other activities.

In War Weapons Weeks, people were encouraged to contribute to the national effort. Colyton's iron gates and railings had already gone for smelting down. On another occasion, the authorities wanted waste paper. We lads collected so much of it that we filled an old cottage behind the chemist's shop. Presumably it was recycled into something more useful.

Less public-spirited were money-making schemes aimed at paying our way into the cinema at Seaton. Picking daffodils in one season and collecting chestnuts in another so that we could sell them door to door or to a greengrocer was innocent enough. There were plenty for everyone, for then daffodils grew in great profusion in the fields.

But, had they known how we duped American soldiers newly arrived in Britain, our efforts would have been less appreciated. The soldiers had just landed in Lions Close Field when we found them. All black they were. We had never seen black men before. And they were hungry. They had plenty of money and didn't know the value of it. We were keen to ensure they didn't find out. We offered to go to Copps bakery for cakes and buns, and we charged them a small fortune. This was my first profitable currency deal.

On Sunday evenings after church we would sometimes walk up the railway line towards Seaton Junction. Curiously, there were always lights flashing in the darkness across the valley. They were carrying messages, we were sure of that. But from whom to whom, and about what? Naturally, we thought they were from spies, and for all we knew they might have been. But we didn't tell anyone. They wouldn't have believed us if we had. More likely, the lights were from troops on manoeuvres. A strange memory, though.

The morning after a plane crash we were at the scene. There were always exciting things to be found. When a German plane came down at Downhayne, we picked up live bullets. At home I had quite an armoury. There was Perspex, too, and you could make good rings from that.

When it was all over, Colyton celebrated as never before. In the square outside the Colcombe Castle, we had a tremendous bonfire. Like everyone else, farmer Reg Virgin enjoyed the occasion. His great red face positively beamed. What he didn't know was how that fire was being kept alive.

We lads knew, for we were raiding faggots from his hayrick. Two at a time the faggots were carried across fields and thrown on the fire. By the end of the evening we had completely cleared the hayrick. How those faggots burned.

When Reg found out what we had done, he wasn't at all pleased. In fact, he was downright angry.

But years later, when I came back to work in Colyton, he was ready to laugh about it. Many were the times we shared our joke to the bewilderment of others around us.

Gerald Goddard, left, went into banking after the war and worked at several branches across the West Country. For the final 14 years of his career he was in charge of the Colyton bank. He has lived in Lyme Regis for more than 30 years.

Queenie Collier

They were long, hard days for a young girl, but my family would just laugh when after tea I would fall asleep, my hands still moving as if I had not stopped milking

I loved dancing. I had loved it from my earliest ballet lessons at school. And that night there was to be a dance in Colyton. I wanted to look my best for it.

My father, though, said that mangel-worzels had to be pulled, a horrible job that meant bending double all day in wet and muddy fields, yanking the blessed things from the ground.

Worse was the yellow-green stain the mangels left on your hands. I pleaded with dad: 'Can't it wait until tomorrow? Surely it can.' But he was adamant. The job had to be done that day. Let them see how hard you work, he said. There's no shame in that.

Gloves were out of the question. They would have shown me up as being soft. In those days, that wouldn't have done at all. So at the end of the day's work I scrubbed and scrubbed my hands, all to no avail. My hands remained grimy and rough and yellow. I would have to go to the dance looking as pretty as I could but with a farm labourer's hands.

I needn't have worried. No-one said anything. No-one pulled

my leg. It was the same for all farmers' daughters. Work in the fields came first.

I was 16 then. It was 1943. We had spent four years worrying about what the war would do to us. The truth was nothing much except backache and grimy hands.

My father had 200 acres or more at Colcombe Abbey, off the Whitford road. When I left school 18 months after the war had started it was to work with him on the farm. Though I was the youngest, and very slight, my labour was needed. Two brothers and a sister had married and left the farm for others in the area. Only my remaining brother Geoff was still on our farm, though he was to leave later. My sister Margie ran the house because mum was unwell.

I wasn't even 14 when I began work. My parents had sent me to Chine School in Seaton but it closed down a month short of the birthday on which I would have left anyway. I didn't mind that they expected me to work on the farm. I had hated school and always loved the outdoors.

I had to get up at 6.30 every morning of the year. What trouble there would have been had the herd not been brought in by the time my father started work half-an-hour later. Geoff and I milked the cows by hand and mucked them out before breakfast, then got on with whatever work was demanded by the changing seasons before milking again in the late afternoon. They were long, hard days for a young girl, but my family would just laugh when after tea I would fall asleep, my hands still moving as if I had not stopped milking.

We had evacuees from London staying with us, two brothers, Charlie and John. A few years ago, Charlie came to see me from his home in Harlow, Essex. We had a cup of tea and a good chat about old times. He still writes every Christmas. Later we had

German prisoners-of-war working on the farm, Joel and Raymond. Mum felt sorry for them. She would make them apple cakes and pies to have with their meals. We never had the slightest trouble. They were nice boys, all of them.

Margie did all the washing. Imagine how dirty our clothes always were. There were no mod cons then, of course. We take it all for granted now, but we had neither electricity nor water in the house.

On our land we had Colcombe Castle, which is now in ruins. It was just across the yard from the house. Water had to be collected in buckets from the well there. It would be heated in the copper before being brought across to the kitchen and tipped into a galvanised bath, where clothes would be washed by hand. Our britches would have been left in soak overnight to tease out the mud. Once clothes were clean, they would be put through the wringer to squeeze out much of the water and hung out to dry. A mangle would be used to remove creases from bedsheets and the like.

Then just as the clean water had been carried in, the dirty water had to be carried out. It would be swilled into the millstream, along with the kitchen waste and all our rubbish. There were no dustbins in those days. The stream would take it all away. The outside toilet emptied into it too. No-one gave a thought to where it was all going and what it was doing.

But we did have a bathroom, where cider barrels had previously been stored. There was no water piped into it, though behind a door off the small downstairs room there was a flush toilet connected to a septic tank. On Saturday night we would fill the tin bath, and my sister and I would follow each other into the same water.

Given the circumstances, it's not surprising that hygiene standards weren't as they are now. Everything took such a lot of effort. Just to keep clean was quite a task. Sometimes it is hard to realise how quickly change has come.

Without power in the kitchen, food was cooked on a stove fuelled by coal and wood and painted with blacklead to keep it smart. A large kettle would simmer in the heat.

It may have been wartime but there was no shortage of food on the farms. We kept pigs and sheep and we had calves for beef; ducks and chickens, too, as well as our own milk, of course. I never drank that. I always hated it, and still do. We would also make our own butter and cheese over at the castle.

Dad would probably kill more pigs and other animals than he was supposed to, but everybody did. We would eat anything an animal offered. Tripe, which many people would no longer know was cow's stomach lining, was quite a delicacy. The chitlings, or small intestines, would be drawn from a pig and they'd be fried. Very tasty, they were. For breakfast we would have what we called blackpots; black pudding to most people. I don't think I would care for them now. And we would use dripping all the time for cooking. The brown layer at the bottom of the dish was lovely on toast.

At night we used candles for light. There was no flicking a switch. In the dark, hairdressing was the most difficult job to do. I would often go to dances with my great friend Margaret Underdown, and afterwards we would stay at the other's house. It was a treat to go home with her because they had electricity. At our house, we had to take it in turns to hold candles while the other did her hair.

I used to like dressing up. It was part of the fun of going out. I suppose I was a bit girlie, despite the rough hands and the hard, physical work. If there was makeup to be had, and we could afford it, Margaret and I would have it. It was mainly Ponds and Max Factor; not the same choice as now. The money came from the wage my dad would pay me and however else I could raise it. Trapping moles and skinning them was one money-making scheme. I would sell the skins for 4d a time to an old chap from Colyton. I would also sell rabbits we caught by long netting. This meant setting up nets around a field and chasing rabbits into them. One of the local butchers called me his little rabbit maid.

We would buy some of our clothes, but a lot were home-made. Nylons were the prized possession, stockings with seams running down the back. They made you look so nice, but you couldn't really get them. Once, Mrs Skinner, a retired farmer's wife, got me two or three pairs. I don't know where they came from; I didn't dare ask. I suppose they must have been from the black market. The first time I wore them to a dance I was the talk of the hall. Everybody crowded around and wanted to know how I'd got them.

I belonged to the Young Farmers and the Young Conservatives, but dancing pleased me the most. I had to be careful what I did because mum and dad were very strict. I was never allowed to go to a pub. The only time I ever did was at Uplyme just before I was married some years after the war, and then I was worried someone would see me and tell mum. Brother Geoff was my ally. He was 10 years older than me and trusted. My parents would tell me to be in by 9 o'clock and he would say they needn't worry because he would see me home. That way I got to stay out later.

When I was 15, I went to dance classes at St Andrew's Hall, and then from 16, to all the dances I could, there and at the town hall; at Kilmington; and at Honiton. We would dance to bands like the Harmony Aces and George Locke and his Edwardians.

Often, we would go first to a Young Farmers' meeting in someone's car because there was a petrol ration for such things as a knowledge bee. Then we would leave the car and walk to the dance, once, I remember from Seaton Junction to Whitford. I loved it all.

The boys were the big attraction, of course. I was a bit of a flirt, I think. Sometimes I would go to a dance with one boy and home with another. Now I'm rather ashamed of my dreadful manners. I would never have anything to do with the Americans, though. I was a bit afraid of them. I stuck with the local farming boys.

For all the fun we had, we were just innocent kids growing up in unusual times.

After she married, Queenie Collier, left, and her husband Ham took over Colcombe Abbey Farm from her parents and ran it for many years. On Ham's death, she sold the farm and moved up the same lane to a new bungalow where she continues to live overlooking Colyton.

Sheliah Taylor

If a German soldier had walked into Colyton I doubt I could have shot him

We had a uniform in the Girls' Training Corps: a white blouse and navy skirt and a little hat. We would meet every Wednesday night at the youth club as part of the war effort.

It was to do with the Home Guard, but for girls and women. They would teach us about guns and show us what we had to do to defend the country if there was an invasion.

But I never did master a gun. I wasn't very good with one. If a German soldier had walked up the lane from Seaton and come into Colyton I doubt I could have shot him, though I suppose I would have been expected to try.

Sheliah Taylor worked at the Symons drapery shop in Market Place as war broke out and later at other shops in Seaton and Exeter. She became British Legion secretary in Colyton and still lives in the town.

Selena Towse

There were bottles and jars everywhere, beautiful containers in blues, greens and reds that carried all the powders, crystals and liquids needed to make medicines

Thankfully it was a moonlit night because we had only a lantern illuminated by a candle to guide us through the lanes. It was around 3am as we trudged two miles to a farm where a child was sick.

My husband had first to make up the medicine at his dispensary in Colyton in response to the emergency. Then we set off on foot because we didn't have a car. In an hour we were at Southleigh and the first dose had been administered. The child would already have been on the road to recovery.

Call it an errand of mercy if you like, but to us it was just a job that had to be done. A child was sick and needed help. As the local pharmacist when there wasn't a doctor in town, my husband had a duty to try to make the child well again. Going out at the dead of night, even if it meant walking a long distance in the dark, was just something he had to do.

We retraced our footsteps to the chemist's shop in Market Place, but there was no time to make up our lost sleep. There was a new day to sap what energy we had left.

Wartime Colyton had its own challenges, but coping with nightly bombing raids as we had done back in the midlands was not one of them. In 1942, we had come from Nottingham, where John had been a director of a chain of pharmaceutical shops. There was death and destruction enough there, but we would look into the sky some nights and from 45 miles away see the red glow of Coventry burning. There, my brother-in-law, a priest, would walk the bombed streets giving out tea and what comfort he could to people who had lost their homes and even their families.

Colyton had become our new home because John had been sick himself with meningitis and had been advised to go to the country for quiet and fresh air. In a pharmaceutical journal, he had seen the chemist's shop for sale. We had stayed at the Colcombe Castle overnight and viewed the shop the following morning. It was in a dreadful state, bad enough to drive me to tears. I couldn't believe that this could possibly be where we would live and work. Both the business and the building had been terribly neglected. The people before us had gone bankrupt and there were even holes in the floor.

But Mrs Cridland, who ran the pub, said the whole town would support us if we moved into the shop. We would never be rich but we would make a living. It was enough to persuade us to buy the business. We were married on the Thursday and in the shop on Saturday, cleaning it and getting it straightened out.

For John it was like starting out again. He had been used to managing a large business. Now he had to do everything for himself, with me as a helper. And there was lots I could do under his direction. In those days, chemists made all they sold. We had machines for making pills and machines for making suppositories. We had to have distilled water for every preparation. We made cod liver oil, bronchial mixtures, medicines for digestive disorders, creams and ointments. We drew water from the pump in the garden and built hives for honey.

I washed the floors every morning at seven ready for the day's work and mended the holes. Gradually, we put the business back together. The shop became what it was supposed to be, less a store for personal products of all sorts and more a pharmacy.

There were bottles and jars everywhere, beautiful containers in blues, greens and reds that carried all the powders, crystals and liquids John needed to make his medicines. They would stand on the mahogany counters and shelves, and beneath them would be the labelled drawers that kept everything you didn't want on show. If you like, it was an old-fashioned pharmacy that was meant not so much for the sale of products that had been bought in but for the preparation of potions and creams that would relieve people's ailments. There were even huge clear bottles containing leeches that were still used to clean up wounds.

Shortages governed our life. Food wasn't the problem. Like everyone else, we found enough of that to eat. It was the scarcity of drugs and health practitioners that was our trouble. To get even a fraction of what he really needed, John had to call on the contacts he had made in his previous business, and he had to become a substitute for the people who would today be taken for granted.

'Mr John', as he became known, would be the doctor, the nurse and the vet when there was none of these specialists on hand. He was the nearest people had and he did his best, often providing services for nothing at all. But it wasn't that people weren't grateful. If they didn't always pay him, they would show their gratitude in other ways. Several times, for example, we found bags of vegetables on the step but never discovered who had left them for us. We often had gifts of venison, too. It was a wonderful life in many ways because everyone helped one another. It was like having a network of mutual support.

In no time at all, the chemist's shop became a health centre. We had a large room at the back of the shop and decided it could be used to provide medical services the town didn't have. One day a week, it became a dentist's consulting room. At first the dentist came from Sidmouth, and when he joined the navy he was succeeded by another dentist from Honiton. On other days, we had an optician and a chiropodist.

There would sometimes be a doctor in town, usually a locum and usually followed by a period when there wasn't a doctor at all. It was the same with vets. Then, doctors and vets were generally men, and men, younger men at least, were required in the armed forces. When they weren't there, we had to manage the best way we could without them.

As well as ministering to sick people from time to time, John was called upon to help farmers with their animals. One night he might be giving medicine to a sick child, the next delivering a calf at a nearby farm. His penicillin creams were in great demand from farmers – and from other people with dermatitis. His udder cream was also used by ladies to rub into their hands. Getting the cream into tubes was my job. You squeezed it in from the bottom and turned up the soft metal, which you pinched together.

It became my job, too, to box and wrap cosmetics so that the local men had something to give their wives and girlfriends at Christmas and birthdays. John didn't take much interest in that, but it all provided useful income. He had his own sense of style, though. Bottles of medicine were sold in white bags, beautifully folded at the top and sealed with red wax.

Within a year of our arrival in Colyton came the Americans. We lived over the shop but there was still room to give them a lounge where they might find some peace and write their letters. There was no stopping their generosity in response. The great number of tins of fruit and meat would go to elderly people in the town.

One night American soldiers were helpful in a different way. John was called to a nursing home in Seaton where a woman was giving birth. She needed a certain drug as an emergency. The soldiers took him in their jeep. Like the sick child to whom we walked at Southleigh, the baby survived. Sadly the mother did not.

John kept a prescription book that can now be seen in the museum at Seaton. Every day he would record people's illnesses and what he had given them. It formed a diary of the times.

Many years later it would come to the rescue of that baby, now a grown woman. She suffered from the same condition as her mother, and John's wartime drug kept her and her baby healthy at her own childbirth.

For the rest of the war and until 1975 Selena Towse continued to help her husband John in his chemist's shop. He died in 1984. She continues to live in Colyton.

Don Hansford

Her washing for the Americans made all the difference to the family budget. What she earned enabled my father to run his little Austin 7 all through the war

Don, second left, with his hard-working mother and family

My mother was off with our old pram again, pushing it briskly to the Americans' camp, a quarter of a mile from home, just outside Beer.

On her return, it would be weighed down by as much dirty washing as she could cram into it.

Most days would be the same. She would collect grimy clothes, wash them, iron them and return them, ready for a new load.

Sometimes I would go with her, lending her a hand as well as a 10-year-old could. If truth be known, I was probably going just for the chewing gum or doughnuts the Americans would give us.

The washing filled our little cottage at Couch Hill, on the Old Beer Road out of Seaton. Steam would cloud the windows and damp would settle on the furniture.

It all had to be done by hand. My mother would heat the water on the blackleaded range fuelled by wood my father would bring home from the farm where he worked. She would tip the clothes into a washtub and beat them with a dolly, a wooden implement with a handle like a spade's but with a domed metal head, holed to allow the pumped water to escape under pressure.

Then she would drain the water from the washed clothes by passing them through the two rollers of a mangle she kept outside the back door. Once dry from the line, they would be ironed and piled up for return to the camp. Such nice uniforms they were.

As hard as it would have been for her, mother's washing for the Americans made all the difference to the family budget. What she earned enabled my father to run his little Austin 7 all through the war. That would have been unusual for a humble farmworker, whose wages wouldn't have stretched to one of the relatively few cars on the road. Only business people and the well-to-do had cars. My father's was his pride and joy. He would drive to his mother's at Burstock, near Broadwindsor in Dorset, and take her shopping. At least, that's what he got a petrol allowance for, presumably because she was in some way dependent on him.

All around us was the evidence of war, and even if we didn't see much action we were affected by it in different ways. We were a close family, who pulled together. Mother and father were hard-working parents who taught my brother, sister and me the virtues of mucking in and making money where we could. Certainly it has stood me in good stead all my life.

Father was in Seaton Home Guard. He had a uniform but not, as far as I remember, a gun. He would stand guard with the others on the cliffs above the town, ready at least to report any invasion threat. A proper Dad's Army they looked.

Below, the beach was defended with tank traps that would have held up the enemy even if it didn't stop them. There were gun emplacements, and down the estuary to Axmouth a line of pillboxes that were sometimes manned.

Up at Beer Quarries, in the cave opposite the one now open to the public, there was a big ammunition dump. Every day, lorries would unload more supplies they had carried from the station at Seaton.

Overhead, we would see the planes carrying Germany's war to the centres of population like Bristol, leaving us largely untouched below.

My father did have a narrow escape one morning on his way to work at Gatcombe Farm. Just in time he saw a bomb device hanging over the track. It had fallen through the trees and become lodged in lower branches. Had he walked into the wire, we would suddenly have been without a father and main breadwinner. As it was, the bomb disposal people made the device safe, and he lived until he was 96.

My only fright was to persist throughout the war – though I saw nothing of the incident that caused it. A German plane was shot down and crashed near Beer. The crew parachuted out and were captured, one near the quarries by a local farmer. From the moment I heard the story, I was nervous. Wherever I went, I felt that somebody was lurking behind me, stalking me. I was always looking over my shoulder for a German who wasn't there.

If I had one anxiety, my parents suffered another – and, I'm afraid, it was all my fault. My excuse is that I was only trying to put money in my pocket and a little more food on the table, as I had been encouraged to do.

Along with other boys, I would climb over the cliff and down the face to grab seagulls' eggs. I was part of a lucrative trade, for I would sell them to the fishmonger in Beer, who boxed them up and sent them to London. For taking the biggest risk I was paid a handsome half-a-crown for each of the eggs. A rich bounty, even if what I was doing scared my parents to death.

At home, we never went short of anything we really needed. We all saw to that. My own contribution was to scavenge and scrump, dig and fish, efforts that sometimes helped others, too.

For during the last two years at school I did almost nothing but raise vegetables. I had to attend assembly in the morning and then report to the school garden. The produce we grew was taken to the headmaster. What happened to it then we never knew. I suppose we hoped it formed part of the Dig for Victory war effort, feeding people in far-off towns, rather than gracing the table of our headmaster. At harvest time, we would be sent to local farms where we would pick potatoes out of the soil.

The Americans' rubbish dump had rich pickings for ourselves. They would throw out so much that we wouldn't waste; tins of cake, for example, and fruit we never saw.

People's allotments provided more for naughty children. We would raid them sometimes for carrots and other vegetables, and of course for apples off the trees.

I particularly liked being near and even on the sea, though I could never swim. I would row out to the trawlers and bring the fishermen to shore. Often they would give me fish for my trouble.

But what I liked doing most was fishing myself from the beach. As the mackerel came into the shallows to feed, I would grab them and net them.

I used to play a bugle and would take it everywhere I went. It came in useful for carrying home the mackerel I had caught for tea.

Don Hansford left school as the war ended. He became a carpet weaver and had three years in the RAF before settling to 40 years as a driver for Express Dairies. In his retirement, he lives in Colyton and collects donation boxes for Devon Air Ambulance.

Ken Underdown

Tall and dark, Werner was special. He was our farm labourer who was delivered by truck every morning and put back behind barbed wire at teatime

Werner Schork was the nicest fellow you could meet. He was a tall, well-built young man of 18 with a pleasant round face. He was always smiling and loved to be with children.

Yet as a German soldier he was our enemy. He had been drafted into an army waging a war for the domination of Europe, a war we were fighting to preserve liberty and self-determination.

He was a prisoner-of-war, detained behind barbed wire. We might have hated him but we didn't. Several PoWs like Werner had worked on my father's land at Road Green Farm, just outside Colyton. They would come and go at haymaking and harvesting and at other times of high activity. Delightful chaps, they all were, though I was apprehensive about them at the start.

They enjoyed getting out of the camps and going to work and were a great help on the farms. Though they were our enemies, nobody showed them any animosity whatever.

Getting help at busy times on the farm at Chantry Bridge had been a problem throughout the war. With most of the young men away fighting, father struggled to keep up with the targets set for him by the WarAg. He just could not get casual labour when it was needed.

After D-Day, the troop camps at Axminster and Honiton held German and Italian prisoners. The ones they could trust were hired out to farmers like my father.

Every morning they were delivered by truck for a day's work on the farm and were collected at tea-time.

Among them all, Werner, tall and dark, was special. Being 12 or 13, I looked up to him and was so pleased my father decided to keep him. It was a shrewd decision because Werner was a farmer's son and knew what he was doing around the farm.

He stayed with us through summer, doing whatever he was told to do day by day and becoming as fond of the family as we were of him. He used to play with us kids, especially football, and would give us anything he could, such as toys he would make from pieces of wood.

Much to the annoyance of my sister and myself, he would be made to take his meals in an outhouse. We thought he should have been allowed to join us at the table, but father would hear nothing of our protests. He continued to insist that Werner ate away from the house, and he was probably right to do so. Anyway, it didn't seem to matter to Werner where he was fed: with great gusto he tucked into all his meals as a lad of his age would do.

Road Green is now nearly 300 acres, but at the outbreak of war it was 60 acres and supported 18 milking cows, with some hay, corn and root vegetables planted for their winter feed. It was one of 35 dairy farms in the Colyton parish, many more than today. Milking, of course, was done by hand. Morning and afternoon my father and mother and their farm labourer collected the milk in buckets and transferred it to churns in the dairy.

Boys parade their rabbiting skill, keeping food on the table

But the war changed life on the farm. Farmers like my father were directed to produce far more. The order came from the Devon War Agricultural Executive Committee, a grandly titled body made up of prominent local farmers, who volunteered to organise others. The WarAg, as it was known, told father how much land he had to plough up for crops like potatoes and corn. He also had to keep pigs because they were cheap to rear for pork, calves for beef and hens, of course, for eggs.

It was all so vital because so many of the Atlantic convoys were not getting through, and people had to be fed. If the farmers couldn't do it, the nation would starve. Dig for Victory was so important that men were not taken off the farms to serve in the forces unless they volunteered.

It worked, too. Productivity increased twofold, and afterwards the government wanted to ensure it didn't slip back. War had made British farming so much more efficient. Because of the schooling I was having, one of my jobs was to fill in all the forms. For along with the extra food that father and the other farmers were producing came officialdom and controls, and we're still stuck with all that.

There was certainly plenty to eat around here. You know what they say: you can never starve a farmer or a rat. There were ways and means of putting food on the table. We were allowed to keep so many eggs and so much milk and kill a pig or two a year for our own use. But when you had killed a pig, what were you supposed to do with all the meat? There weren't fridges and freezers and you couldn't salt it all down. So, unknown to the authorities, you let someone else have some. It would be smuggled out of the farm by car in great secrecy. Woe betide you if you were caught. Then when someone else slaughtered an animal he would let you have some of his meat. Food found its way around the countryside like this, a quarter of a pig here, a few joints there, or perhaps some eggs. Favours, you might say, for family and friends.

Some people were in the black market too. More meat than should have been the case went under the counter at butchers' shops, and the farmer would get a backhander, though I'm sure we weren't involved. That way the butcher would also make a bit of money and his regular customers would benefit, too. Everybody was happy and nobody went hungry.

Rabbits were another source of good food. They would reach the dinner plate in all sorts of ways. At harvesting time, everybody knew there were rabbits to be had, especially the boys. Word would go around at school that so-and-so farmer would be cutting his corn and they would hurry to the field after lessons.

The corn would be cut by a binder moving around the field, from the hedges inwards. A smaller and smaller area of corn would be left in the middle, surrounded by boys wielding sticks and men with shotguns farther out towards the hedges. As the rabbits fled, often 100 or so of them, the boys would beat them with sticks to slow them down and then catch them by hand. They would hoist them by their rear legs and deliver a rabbit punch to the back of the neck. Any that escaped would be shot by the men. Yes, young boys would have been running about a field in which guns were being fired. It wouldn't be allowed today, that's for sure. When the killing was all over, the boys would often be given two or three rabbits apiece by the farmer and they would run off home with the next day's dinner or to sell them to butchers for pocket money.

Whether it was pigs or rabbits, there weren't any shortages of meat. Compared with the rations endured by people in the cities, this was a land of plenty.

It was also a happy place. We children enjoyed growing up through the war. There was always so much to do, and sometimes a little excitement, too. I still have the smell in my nostrils whenever I think of the German plane that crashed through three hedges at Downhayne, not far from our farm. We got there as soon as possible to see what had happened, and the smell of the hot metal and burning fuel has never left me.

The arrival of evacuees from London had made the first impact of war on Colyton. I was in St Andrew's choir, which was augmented by some of them. We all got on very well together. But how good we were, I shudder to think. For in the winter, because of the blackout, we practised in the dark, tutored by an elderly organist who had few teaching skills. He would sit high up in the organ loft and shout down 'Rubbish, rubbish' whenever we failed to please him.

The evacuees had doubled the number of children in Colyton. They carried on as St Jude's School in the town hall and later, after some had returned home, the remainder integrated with the local children at the council school. By the end of the war most, if not all, had gone back to London, but some became attached to the town and stayed or returned.

None of the children from this school was billeted at the farm but later two girls from Dulwich College in London came to stay with us. They were well-to-do sisters who spoke very nicely. They lived at the farm for no more than six months but it turned out to be a crucial time for me.

Along Horse Lane from the farm was Colyton's swimming pool. Men and women, and boys and girls, were admitted at different times. But young boys were allowed in with older girls.

One day I fell in at the deep end. A number of older girl evacuees were there, including the two staying with us.

I can still see the bubbles rising above me as I sank to the bottom. I might well have drowned but for one of the girls jumping in to my rescue. She hauled me out and I spluttered back to life. A bigger debt no-one owed our wartime visitors.

We never saw our evacuees again but many years later Werner returned to see us. At the end of the war he had moved on to a farm at Whitford and made friends with a lad of his own age called Reg James. They kept in touch and Reg would let us know how Werner was doing.

Then sadly Reg died, and Werner sent a wreath to his funeral. Since then he has never failed to send birthday and Christmas presents to Reg's widow, Nancy.

He hadn't been able to travel to England for the funeral but has on two other occasions and once he called on us at the farm.

It was a wonderful surprise to see him.

Ken Underdown attended agricultural college after leaving Colyton Grammar School. He later took over his father's farm where he still helps his son in his own retirement. For 10 years he was churchwarden at St Andrew's.

Werner Schork

A little light shone in the sky. Spring was coming and my number was chalked against the name of Mr Gardner. A friendship was to begin that would last my whole life

The snow fell relentlessly. It was Christmas and my 20th birthday, but there wasn't much to celebrate, this being my third birthday in captivity. I desperately wanted to go home to Germany.

By day we prisoners were put to work clearing the snow. By night there would be yet another game of cards to pass the time until lights-out.

I lay awake at night staring at the same moon and stars I could see at home. Somehow they seemed to draw me closer to the family I had left behind. How I yearned for the freedom I had never enjoyed as a young man.

That winter, soon after the end of the war, was miserable. I had liked working the previous summer for Mr Underdown on the edge of Colyton. He was a kind and friendly man and I enjoyed playing with his children.

But now I was back in the camp at Honiton, being trucked to farms for a day's work here and a day's work there and never getting to know anyone. My youth was being wasted, achieving nothing, going nowhere, learning so little.

Werner Schork as a young soldier in the south of France 1944

Already it seemed a long time since my call-up in March 1944. I had gone to serve in the Panzerjaegern, or armoured corps, and been sent, along with about 45 young men from the training unit, to Bordeaux in occupied south-west France.

By August we were retreating. My regiment was transferred to Besancon, south of Strasbourg, in north-east France, during the Allied offensive that followed the D-Day invasion. There we defended the town for four days before surrendering. My capture in September began a four-year odyssey of prison camps and farm labour.

In Honiton, the days were passing slowly and cold for the 150 prisoners, and now there was a little light in the sky, some warmth when the sun shone. Spring was on its way and my number was chalked against the name of Mr Gardner. A friendship was to begin that would last my whole life.

That day the lorry took me to Whitford. My welcome was a real one. Mr Gardner had children and workers much my own age and we soon became friends.

The work would be divided between me and Ronald Bright, a lad a year older than me who came to work on a motor bike. Sometimes we would spend the whole day together, eating our lunch as we sat on the feed-racks in the stables.

And, as from Colyton, the truck collected me again, usually for a meal of stew: potatoes with some meat, peas, beans and carrots. With it, there were two slices of bread. Afterwards, we played cards before a night's sleep. Sometimes, instead of the stew, we were given fish and chips.

Ronald and I stayed friends even when Mr Gardner surprised me with an invitation to live at the farm, an arrangement sanctioned by the authorities. Needless to say, I jumped at the chance: it was so much nicer at the farm than in the camp. I moved in and they

Top: Taking refreshment on the farm at Whitford.
Bottom: Werner, second from left, standing, at the prisoner-
of-war camp in America 1946

treated me like a son. But now I would eat with the family and Ronald would stay out in the stables at lunchtime. I found this difficult, and no doubt he did too. But one Saturday he took me on his motor bike to a speedway meeting at Exeter. It may have been his way of saying he understood.

On my free Saturdays I often accompanied Reg James, Mr Gardner's son-in-law, as he collected milk churns left at the roadside by nearby farmers. When we finished, we would go to the local pub for a couple of pints. No-one showed me any animosity.

At the camp, I had to register the number of hours I worked. This was because Mr Gardner had to pay the government for every hour at the same rate he paid English workers. But when I worked more than the usual eight hours in the day I didn't tell anyone. Mr Gardner would give me money and gifts.

Sadly, nothing lasts for ever. My days at Whitford came to an abrupt and tragic end when Mr Gardner died unexpectedly. It wouldn't have been right for me to live at the farm then, so after eight of the more enjoyable months of the war period I was back in the camp.

Later, I had a chance to live and work at another farm, but it wasn't the same. There was no running water, no electricity, everything was a mess and the farmer was workshy. Though he was a preacher at the Methodist church in Colyton, he wasn't very Christian. He would even take my dinner plate from me if he thought his wife had given me a bigger portion of food.

That was where I was at the next Christmas, my 21st birthday. But it was back at the Gardners' where I celebrated with coffee and cakes, having borrowed Ronald's motor bike to get me there.

By now it was almost 1948. I had been a prisoner since 1944. Home in Munzenberg, north of Frankfurt, seemed a distant but happy memory. It was there that I had been born on a small farm, the first child of Otto and Ottilie Schork. My upbringing had been like that of most other German children as Adolf Hitler rose to power.

At 10 I had joined the Jungwolk, the children's branch of the Hitler Youth, of which I was later to become a junior leader in my village. By my call-up I had qualified as a painter and decorator and later in 1943 went to work in occupied Poland. Little did I know how long it would be before I had another birthday and Christmas at home.

At my 17th birthday I was a security guard and general workman at Posen in Poland. By my 18th I was a prisoner-of-war. With 350 other prisoners I had been trucked south through France to the Mediterranean and shipped to Algeria. There in a hot, dusty desert prison camp my birthday went without being noticed.

Next month, in January 1945, I found myself in the United States after a three-week voyage, being deloused before a long train journey to a military camp in Georgia. From there, packed in articulated trucks, we were taken every day to a giant freight depot where we loaded and unloaded weapons and machine-guns for overseas. We also taught one another our respective languages. The supervisor wanted to learn German. My fellow prisoners and I wanted to learn English. So we spent much of our time on language lessons.

We got 12 cents an hour in camp currency for our work, and I used my money to buy bottles of beer from the canteen to celebrate my 19th birthday, the first Christmas of peacetime in Europe.

After a year in the US we were told we were to be released. We were put on board ship for Liverpool and then a train for a camp near Coventry. We thought this was to be a break before the journey back to Germany. After a few days we had to march about three miles with heavy rucksacks to the nearest station. We thought we were travelling to the east coast and on to Germany, but instead the train took us to Tiverton in Devon and another labour camp.

A few weeks later I was on Mr Underdown's farm learning to milk cows by hand and mucking out the cowsheds, eating three sandwiches from the camp for my lunch sitting on a crate in the feed room and having our dry, black tea leaves brewed up by the farmer's wife. It was to be nearly another two years before I would get home.

Only then, in March 1948, did my odyssey finally end. I was sent back to the camp in Tiverton, where we gave in our prisoner's clothes and laundry and were put on a train to Harwich. Even then I was frightened we might end up in a French port and another labour camp. But to my great joy we landed in the Hook of Holland. Soon we were back in Germany where I was given my release papers.

I had often felt that I was being treated not like a human being with feelings but more like an object that could be pushed around from place to place. The French PoWs who had worked on the family farm had been released straightaway at the end of the war, but for us the delay had extended for three years. No-one who hasn't experienced it can really understand what it means to have one's beautiful youth spent at war and as a prisoner.

The last part of my journey home took me through the ruins that were now Germany. The devastation greatly saddened me. From the station, there was just a short walk but it took a very long time as one person after another greeted me warmly. I was home.

It was wonderful to be back in Munzenberg, even though my father had died a soldier in Russia. After so many years being forced to work on other people's farms, I had to throw myself into work on the family farm kept going by my mother, sister and grandfather.

There was little time to think of the past but I never forgot the happier times of my capitivity .

Many years later, in 1990, my wife Elfriede and I were to meet Nancy and Reg when they took a holiday in Germany, and the following year we were invited back to meet all the people who had been so kind to me.

How the tears flowed when we left.

Werner Schork worked to expand the family farm. He continues to live at Munzenberg in what became West Germany until the Berlin Wall fell in 1989. At 80 he wrote the 3,000 words on which this story was based.

David Hurford

His days would have been endured in the noise and terror of battle. Back home, in the village where he had grown up, it couldn't have been more different

Not long before Trooper 'Jasper' Hard fought his last battle in northern Italy, I stood on the lawn and watched a blanket of aircraft smother the sky.

You could hardly see space between the bombers and fighters as they roared overhead for what seemed like hours on three successive nights.

The invasion my parents would have feared had never happened and now never would happen. This was not the defeat that would have enslaved us. This was victory in the making. 'That job's on,' somebody said, reflecting on local intelligence. From all the movements of troops and equipment, people had deduced that a big offensive was taking shape.

We were excited but also anxious. In a few days we might have a great victory to cheer, yet much might still go wrong. We just had to trust in the generals.

In Italy, Trooper Hard had been fighting with the Eighth Army as it pursued the German forces up the east coast. The Gustav Line south of Rome had been broken in May and now the British, the Poles and the Canadians were threatening the Gothic Line intended to hold the Allies out of the north.

Trooper Hard's regiment had been seconded to the 2nd Polish Corps. For two days they fought to overcome stern German resistance before capturing Ancona, a port on the Adriatic coast.

And there he died, Trooper Hard, 306214, Royal Horse Guards, son of Charles Henry and Sarah Hard from my own village of Northleigh. He wasn't ever to wear the Maid of Warsaw, a privilege his regiment earned from the Poles for their heroism in that battle.

His latter days would have been endured in the noise and terror of battle, in the muck and dust, amid flying bullets and exploding mortar shells. His comrades would have fallen around him, and exhaustion would have become his second enemy. Still he would have fought on to the next objective until called upon to make the ultimate sacrifice.

Back home, in the village where he had grown up as the son of the landlords of the New Inn pub, it couldn't have been more different. Farmers and their families continued their quiet lives, now more optimistic about what their futures might be. I was not yet 12, running about the fields, getting into mischief as boys of that age do. Life was all fresh air and free of care.

By now, many of the evacuees would have returned to the cities, but Farwood Barton, our Victorian farmhouse on the edge of the village, was still full of people.

Early in the war, evacuees had come and gone, and the local school had doubled in size. But, in September 1942, two families, the Philpotts from Croydon and the Crouches from New Malden in Surrey, had arrived and stayed. It was to be a happy time for us all.

Had he known it, Mr Crouch might have been following Trooper Hard's campaign. He was an avid radio listener and brought us all our news. He told us the Eighth had landed in Sicily and then in mainland Italy, and his announcements, like the others about Allied victories, were greeted with satisfaction.

An earlier Eighth Army triumph had even caused the medieval bells of the village church to ring out. Church bells had remained silent everywhere; they were to be rung only in the event of an invasion and then to warn people of their fate. But prime minister Winston Churchill regarded Mongomery's defeat of Rommel at El Alamein as the turning point of the war and ordered bells to ring in celebration.

Until two of the Crouch boys were called up, there had been 11 children in the house, including my three siblings and myself.

To people today, that may seem an unlikely number of children to be in one place at the same time, out of school. But then the gathering was no larger than some families without any guests, families without the sort of facilities we had. There was no electricity, but we had running water. In fact, we had a fully-functioning bathroom and two other flush toilets. The two evacuee families shared a kitchen and we had our own. Altogether there were eight bedrooms rather than the two or three most had. So we were fortunate.

And everyone got on famously. In fact, the Crouch family stayed in the area after the war and one of the children, Nellie, remains a cornerstone of the Seaton Catholic Church.

Our Christmases together were always special. Food was never short for people in the countryside. When we killed a pig we would share it with the next farm. My brother and I would haul the half-carcase across the fields and would be given such a welcome it would even include chocolate.

Come December there were the turkeys to pluck, and then the great day itself would arrive. The table in the middle of our huge kitchen would groan with food. While people in the cities made do with whatever they could get, we had a feast. Mrs Crouch was in her element. She was a former chef, and her puddings and pies were to be marvelled at.

As the war ground on, Farwood Barton became a target for army training. Troops would often be on exercise down the lanes, but on one occasion the farmhouse was attacked by a group of soldiers and defended by another. They crept through the buildings, taking up new positions. One chap crawling among the cattle came face to face with the bull tied up in a stall. The bull appeared eager to know what was going on and the soldier looked frightened to death. Amid the frenzy, rifles fired blank cartridges. How they decided who had the upper hand was anybody's guess. But apparently it was the attackers who won the day and who took the defenders as prisoners. Nobody minded what games the army had to play on exercise or what inconvenience soldiers caused. People would have done anything to help them win the war.

One local RAF pilot was a bit naughty, though. On his way back from bombing raids he would take a diversion to buzz his parents' house at Farway. He would bring this thundering great aircraft low down the valley, presumably to assure them he was home again. Sadly, he was later to lose his life over the Channel.

By 1944, as Trooper Hard was liberating Italy, the emphasis at home had also switched from defence to attack. The aircraft flying overhead were softening up the Germans for D-Day, the Americans who had been billeted in the area had moved to the coast ahead of the landings in France and the Home Guard was soon to be disbanded.

For a year, the news grew steadily better. Then came the surrender. Northleigh's ancient church filled for the thanksgiving, and 40 or

50 of the local men, who had been called upon to do little more than guard Honiton Tunnel at night, went back into Home Guard uniform for the victory parade.

At last, all their drill practice paid off. They marched as they had never done before, the creases in their trousers as sharp as a pin.

It was many years after that joyous parade before Trooper Hard's death was honoured in his home village. The memorial in the church listed 10 men who had died in the First World War, including two brothers who had worked on our farm, one of whose deaths was not notified to his family until Armistice Day.

But Trooper Hard, a farmworker until his call-up at 18, had been the only local man to die in the Second World War and nobody had put up a memorial to him.

After the Service of Remembrance in 1970 I told Major Smith of the omission. It was now 26 years since Jasper had lost his life in defence of his country. My own destiny had been to farm Farwood Barton, like my father before me. My life would be spent on the land where I had been born.

Major Smith had come to live in the village and was now treasurer of the church, as I would later become before my many years as churchwarden. He spluttered with incredulity. Then, in his soft, upper-class accent, exclaimed: 'Never been put up, you say. We will remedy that before next Remembrance Sunday.'

And they did.

The new white memorial tablet on the north wall of the church beneath the fallen of the Great War read:

'Trooper Charles H J Hard, Royal Horse Guards,

Italy, 30th August 1944.

His name liveth for ever more.'

'Jasper' was just 20, hardly yet a man and not many years older than me, when he died a hero on foreign soil as I began to learn how to look after the grass and the cattle.

Peace had come to us both in such different ways.

1939 – 1945
TROOPER CHARLES H.J. HARD.
ROYAL HORSE GUARDS.
ITALY 30TH AUGUST 1944.
HIS NAME LIVETH FOR EVERMORE.

Postscripts

St Jude's headmaster George Lancaster returned to London with his school after the war, but retired with his wife to Colyton soon afterwards. Later he served as clerk to the parish council for 16 years.

Cecil Day-Lewis worked during the war as a propagandist for the Ministry of Information. He was poet laureate from 1968 until his death in 1972.

Muriel Turl died on 3 December 2006, four days after telling her dramatic story. She was 78.

Herbert Breiter survived the war, earning a number of decorations including the European-African-Middle Eastern Campaign Medal with five bronze service stars. He was discharged from the US Army on 30 November, 1945, and died in 1998.

Charles Henry Jasper Hard lies buried in Ancona War Cemetery, north-east Italy, where the graves are tended by the Commonwealth War Graves Commission.

Acknowledgments

This book could not have been written without the wholehearted support of the many men and women who raided their memories of times long ago to have recorded in someone else's words the stories of their youth spent while their country was at war. My thanks go to them. Deservedly, their contributions will form part of East Devon's social history.